APOSTOLIC FAITH IN AMERICA

Edited by

THADDEUS D. HORGAN

WILLIAM B. EERDMANS PUBLISHING COMPANY
GRAND RAPIDS, MICHIGAN
FOR
COMMISSION ON FAITH AND ORDER
NATIONAL COUNCIL OF THE CHURCHES OF CHRIST
IN THE U.S.A.

Copyright © 1988 by Commission on Faith and Order, NCCCUSA
475 Riverside Dr., Room 872, New York, NY 10115-0050 (212) 870-2569

First published 1988 for the Commission on Faith and Order by
William B. Eerdmans Publishing Co.
255 Jefferson Ave. S.E., Grand Rapids, Mich. 49503

The Commission on Faith and Order and the publisher wish to
acknowledge the assistance of the Commission staff in producing this
volume:
  Brother Jeffrey Gros, director
  Stefanie Yova Yazge
  Alexandra Brown
  Barbara Henninges

Library of Congress Cataloging-in-Publication Data

Apostolic faith in America / edited by Thaddeus D. Horgan.

    p.   cm.
  ISBN 0-8028-0415-2
  1. Church—Apostolicity. 2. Christian sects—United States.
I. Horgan, Thaddeus D. (Thaddeus Daniel). II. National Council of
the Churches of Christ in the United States of America. Commission
on Faith and Order.
BV601.2.A67   1988
262'.72—dc19   88-16374
                                       CIP

Contents

Foreword

In 1854, a Swiss Reformed immigrant to the United States, Philip Schaff, gave some lectures in Germany under the title *Amerika*. The budding church historian there described his new country as offering "a motley sampler of all Church history, and the results it has thus far attained." Since that time, yet further episodes have been embroidered into the sampler, with the arrival of Slavic and Levantine Orthodox, Hispanic Catholics, and Korean Protestants (to name only some) and as such indigenous developments as Pentecostalism have taken place. A Christian sampler has to contain a golden thread: the apostolic faith. Leaders in the current NCCC study on the apostolic faith rightly began by trying to discern that thread in the past and present lives of their own and each others' denominational traditions. Sometimes the tarnished thread needs burnishing. Certainly the hope must be that, as a result of the attention now being given to the theme in so many quarters, the golden hue will become increasingly prominent as the Christian story unfolds in this country and future scenes are worked into its pictorial record.

Schaff also envisaged America as "a Phoenix grave not only of all European nationalities but also of all European churches and sects, of Protestantism and Romanism. . . . Out of the mutual conflict of all, something wholly new will gradually arise." The wonderful creature was not yet apparent to Dietrich Bonhoeffer who, during his visits in the 1930s, wryly observed that "it has been given to the Americans less than any other nation of the earth to realize on earth the visible unity of the Church of God." No doubt Bonhoeffer's idea of unity was somewhat limited by a European, Constantinian model. But it has to be admitted that American Christians still have a long way to go in realizing an appropriate pattern of church unity. Agreement in the apostolic faith will in any case be an indispensable element in whatever is achieved.

One feature that is not stressed by name in the description of the national character and context in the first chapter of the present book is American pragmatism. This characteristic will ensure that attention to the apostolic faith does not remain at the level of words to the exclusion of deeds. In the early years of the international Life and Work movement, it used to be said that "Doctrine divides, service unites." Today some would claim that the reverse is the case: the churches are converging in their doctrinal statements, while social action is proving divisive among Christians. The current NCCC project encourages exploration of appropriate ways in which the apostolic faith may be simultaneously and credibly confessed in both words and deeds. The Christian confession is made before God and before our fellow human beings, *coram Deo* and *coram hominibus*. The profession and enactment of our faith has doxological, evangelistic, and ethical dimensions, and it is a matter of finding the proper correspondences so that there may be substantive identity between what is confessed in the different modes of worship, proclamation, and life. The NCCC Faith and Order work is clearly marked by a concern for these correspondences.

Another trait that strikes the relative newcomer to these shores is the participatory character of American society. In terms of process, we may hope that the Apostolic Faith project will engage study and work groups in the local congregations. Help is provided by the excellent guide, *Confessing One Faith— The Origins, Meaning and Use of the Nicene Creed—Grounds for a Common Witness* (Cincinnati: Forward Movement Publications). Engagement at the local level is vital to the search for that unity among Christians which is itself a constituent in the apostolic faith: Paul expects Christians to "glorify with one heart and one voice the God and Father of our Lord Jesus Christ" (Rom. 15:5-6); united testimony is needed if the world is to believe in the divine mission of the Son (John 17:20-23); unreconciled Christians can hardly witness to a gospel of reconciliation (2 Cor. 5:17-20). In the United States, the discovery and attainment of appropriate forms of Christian unity is a particularly difficult process: Christians are rightly suspicious of the "merger" model that smacks of big business, and they fear a denominational, or even an ecumenical, bureaucracy that would remain out of touch with local congregations. It is to be hoped that local engagement in the Faith and Order project will contribute to the emergence of forms of church unity that are national in scope while firmly rooted in the particular places.

The NCCC project rightly makes much of the American context for confessing the apostolic faith. It is, however, important to be aware that the national study is closely linked to the global effort "Towards the Common Expression of the Apostolic Faith Today" on the part of the Commission on Faith and Order of the World Council of Churches. Awareness of the wider project will help to counteract any tendencies either to isolationism or to imperialism. Positively put, the American study can make a contribution at the world level precisely because our history and situation offer (to vary the images from Schaff's sampler and Phoenix grave) something of a "microcosm" of the complex Christian Tradition and a "crucible" from which may perhaps emerge new patterns of Christian unity.

In return, we may profit from outside assistance. The WCC decision to make the Nicene-Constantinopolitan creed "the theological basis and methodological tool" of its apostolic faith study has already helped to put a trinitarian stamp on the American *Confessing One Faith*. The American constitutional background in Enlightenment deism brings an endemic tendency to minimize the specific character of God's self-revelation as received in catholic Christianity. Stimulated, on the one hand, by feminist critiques of trinitarian nomenclature, and on the other by the strong witness made by American Christians of Orthodox allegiance to the tripersonal being of God, renewed attention to the doctrine and reality of the Holy Trinity may help the united recovery of the liberating character of the nature and works of God, and of faith as participation in the eternal communion of the one whom Jesus called Father, of the divine Son himself, and of the Holy Spirit whom they promised. Such participation in the divine communion may not be without its outworkings in that unity-in-diversity and freedom-in-service which the life of the church is meant to signify in the world.

The Divinity School   GEOFFREY WAINWRIGHT
Duke University
Ascension Day 1988

Introduction:

CONFESSING THE APOSTOLIC FAITH IN AMERICA

The Commission on Faith and Order of the National Council of Churches has responded to the 1982 worldwide Faith and Order movement's "call to the Churches to the goal of visible unity in one faith, one eucharistic fellowship expressed in worship and in common life in Christ in order that the world may believe."[1] The papers here are the result of the Apostolic Faith Study Groups' work. They were prepared with a consciousness of the context in which our churches live, confess faith, minister, and seek to be one.

The North American context is unique. This needs emphasis because the great difference between the North American and European experience is not always acknowledged. Many churches have come into being solely within the complex American experience. For many Christians in the U.S. their living memory and histories as churches do not include a European past. But a European connection may be in the future as daughter churches are established there.

The North American experience is of particular significance because of the considerable influence of many U.S. churches in Latin America and the Carribean. Both mainline and evangelical/pentecostal churches are engaged in witness and mission throughout the southern hempishere, where the European connection more and more is seen as "heritage" rather than current relationship. Many mainline churches have their historic roots in Europe and are in communion with their European counterparts. But adjustments required by the principle "unity with diversity" are not always easily perceived, much less made. The

---

1. *Towards Visible Unity*, vol. 2, Faith and Order Paper 113 (Geneva: World Council of Churches, 1982), pp. 44-46.

apparent tensions within the Roman Catholic Church between the U.S. church and Rome seem to exemplify this. Apostolicity itself is one reason for the great diversity that exists among the churches in North America. Many came into being because of struggles to achieve a lived fidelity to the gospel. Current trends within the churches, no matter how they are labeled, are explained and justified by fidelity to the apostolic faith.

For these reasons the following papers have been developed by the National Council of Churches' Commission on Faith and Order Apostolic Faith Study Groups. Specific persons were given the task of writing them, but they are the result of input and dialogue by all in the Study Groups.[2] They are published to

---

2. The members of the two study groups responsible for these papers are:

The American Context:

Gabriel Abdelsayed, Coptic Orthodox Church, Jersey City, NJ;
Juan Acosta, Episcopal, National City, CA;
Donald Bruggink, Reformed Church in America, Holland, MI;
Donald Dayton, Wesleyan Holiness, Lombard, IL;
Thomas Fitzgerald, Greek Orthodox, Brookline, MA;
Thaddeus Horgan, Roman Catholic, Graymoor, NY;
Thomas Hoyt, Jr., Christian Methodist Episcopal, Hartford, CT;
Lewis Lancaster, Presbyterian Church, USA, Atlanta, GA;
Lauree Hersch Meyer, Church of the Brethren, Oakbrook, IL;
Cecil Robeck, Society for Pentecostal Studies, Pasadena, CA;
David Shannon, National Baptist Convention, USA, Atlanta, GA

Dimensions of the Apostolic Faith:

Arten Ashjian, Armenian Church in America, New York, NY;
Craig Atwood, Moravian Church in America, Bethlehem, PA;
Emmanuel Clapsis, Greek Orthodox, Brookline, MA;
Mary Ann Donovan, Roman Catholic, Berkeley, CA;
Thomas Finger, Mennonite Church, Chicago, IL;
Dean Freiday, Friends General Conference, Manasquan, NJ;
Mark Heim, American Baptist, Newton Center, MA;
James Jorgenson, Orthodox Church in America, Livonia, MI;
Samuel Nafzger, Lutheran Church, Missouri Synod, St. Louis, MO;
William Rusch, Evangelical Lutheran Church in America, Chicago, IL;
Gilbert Stafford, Church of God, Anderson, IN;
Clyde Steckel, United Church of Christ, New Brighton, MN;
Marjorie Suchocki, United Methodist Church, Washington, DC;
George Vandervelde, Christian Reformed Church, Toronto, ON.

highlight the quest for a lived fidelity to the apostolic faith by American Christians that our multiplicity of churches does not always project. We also wish to share the American church experience with others of different cultures and historical heritages so that they might come to know the churches in North America better.

These papers likewise contribute to the larger study of the issue carried on by the World Council of Churches. In this light the contextual circumstance of Christian experience in the United States is first set forth. Then brief appreciations of apostolicity found in the ancient churches, the magisterial Reformation churches, and the World Council of Churches' studies are offered. At that point a reflection on apostolicity in the American context is inserted to set the scene for presentations on nine American churches' expressions of the apostolic faith. Studies on the world level are based on the experience of the ancient churches and the magisterial Reformation churches as they are found in Europe. Finally, recommendations for advancing this study are made. These were arrived at after lengthy and arduous discussion over a three-year period.

The quest for Christian unity is an obligation because of Christ's will that his followers be one (John 17:21-23). It requires commitment and is a task. What is presented here is one fruit of a labor that representatives of North American churches have undertaken. Its conclusions look to the future. The task is begun, but hardly accomplished.

THADDEUS DANIEL HORGAN, SA

CHARACTERISTICS OF THE AMERICAN CONTEXT

THADDEUS HORGAN, SA, and THOMAS HOYT, JR.

CONTEXTUALIZATION

When one reads Paul's sermon given at Pisidian Antioch during his first missionary journey (Acts 4:16-41), it is apparent that it is addressed to a Jewish audience. The idea of the covenant and the fulfillment of promises to David dominate the text. These promises were fulfilled not only in David but also in Jesus, risen from the dead. Paul cites two well-known messianic texts, Psalm 2:7 and Isaiah 55:3, to demonstrate the point.

When Paul preaches at Athens, however, his hearers are not Jews (Acts 17:22-31). His approach is different. The universalism of God's rule over all reality is his theme. As long as Paul spoke of this he held his hearers. When he introduced ideas of resurrection, he encountered objections. This was not surprising then; nor is it now. But today theologians, indeed all church leadership, have taken heightened notice of the context within which faith is proclaimed, appreciated, witnessed to, commented on, and lived.

Contextualization refers to the historico-cultural rootedness of the experience and expression of faith.[1] This is why Paul used different motifs in his preaching. In explaining faith today we speak of theologies. What is implied is context. For example, there are multiple liberation theologies: American black theology reflects black American experience, which is not the Caribbean black experience nor the South African black one.

---

1. See Robert J. Schreiter, *Constructing Local Theologies* (Maryknoll, N.Y.: Orbis Books, 1985), esp. chaps. 3 and 4, for a discussion of contextualization.

Latin American liberation theology refers not only to rootedness but also to the method of "doing theology."

Contextualization involves the signs and symbols that express a society's values, communicate their meaning, and express to "outsiders" the group's identity. Identifying these signs and symbols in a living society is complex. Their meaning constantly changes. But identifying their significance and their influence at a given moment contributes to one's appreciation and understanding of particular issues. Contextualization focuses on when one reflects, writes, or speaks out of a particular heritage.

This juncture sometimes is called a society's culture. For some, culture is the source of a people's language, art, music, architecture, and way of living. For others it is the sum total of a people's distinctiveness that explains their art, music, or dance. However one defines it, cultural expressions tell us how a people look at life and perceive its meaning. Culture indicates the dynamics of change for a people. Since no human society is static, contextualization embraces its present and past, and also serves as a window looking toward its future.

North America, like western Europe, is frequently described as post-Christian. In view of this, the manner in which one faithfully witnesses to and expresses Christian faith becomes a burning issue because western European/North American cultures have been Christianity's vehicle and context for centuries. The current context forces us to consider anew how we confess, or should confess, faith. Is it as Paul did in Pisidian Antioch, or in Athens, or in other ways? In a recent article, "Contextual Theology and a New Ecumenism," Mark Ellingsen concludes that the issue is an essential concern for mainline and evangelical Christians to face, and to face together.[2]

THE DISTINCTIVE NORTH AMERICAN CONTEXT

Can one speak of a North American context for confessing the apostolic faith—or of rejecting it? The question should be put

2. *Christian Century*, 13-20 August 1986, pp. 713-14.

both ways. The facts are before us. Many North Americans are enthusiastic proclaimers of the faith. The United States has produced more evangelizers for its own peoples than most other nations. North American churches, particularly the evangelical and pentecostal bodies, are outstanding in their zeal for overseas evangelizing ministries, notably in Latin America and the Caribbean. Never has Christ been proclaimed more. There is even an "electronic church" for those who do not identify with a local congregation. Yet an estimated ninety million Americans, or approximately 35 percent of the population, claim no faith affiliation! Many see this not so much as a rejection of faith as a lack of clear identity on the part of a Christian with a particular tradition.

Denominational labels have blurred the importance of confessing the apostolic faith classically, that is, according to a given heritage and ecclesial tradition. The United States has more than three hundred Protestant denominations; some single storefront congregations, others multimillion-member churches. The result is that there are Americans who neither know nor are capable of reciting the *Creed* but whose self-consciousness is that they are definitely Christian.

Despite the Protestant image of the United States, the Roman Catholic Church is its largest denomination, with fifty-two million registered members, or 24 percent of the total population.[3] There are twenty-one Eastern Orthodox and Oriental Orthodox churches, whose combined membership constitute 6 percent of the nation's total population. Another 4 percent are Jewish, and close to 5 percent of Americans are Muslims. Despite all their evangelization efforts most churches claiming converts have to admit that the vast majority do not come from unbelief, but from another church! What do these things tell us about confessing faith today in America apart from the obvious, namely that the context is complex?

One can approach the matter from a variety of perspectives. History, however, seems best because our concern is the ancient apostolic faith. But there is no one religious history of North

---

3. For an overview of the Roman Catholic Church's history see James Hennessy, SJ, *American Catholics: A History of the Roman Catholic Community in the United States* (New York: Oxford University Press, 1981).

America. There are histories, many of completely opposite experience. In this chapter we will primarily, but not exclusively, consider the European American and American black experiences to demonstrate this point. For white Europeans who came in search of religious freedom the history of the Christian religion in North America immediately brings to mind "immigration." Some fled Catholic tyrannies; others the newly established Protestant ones. Whether one was a Puritan in New England or a Roman Catholic in Maryland accounts for the early diversity of religious experience among whites in North America.[4] Both the immigration of whites and of Hispanics continues in American society. But the reason for both today is no longer religious; it is more likely political or economic.

Black immigration, especially from the Caribbean, is a post–World War II phenomenon. However, for African-Americans the history of the Christian religion in North America immediately brings to mind slavery, segregation, and discrimination. Initially they came in chains. Theirs was not a search for religious freedom but a struggle to survive in a hostile society made intolerable by Christians and non-Christians alike. They were not even evangelized until it became clear to many in the church that such evangelization would not change the status of converted slaves. Many who came to America in search of religious freedom too often found themselves acting in unfreedom toward those in their midst who were Native Americans (Indians) and blacks.

The experience of the early white European immigrant Christian did shape many elements of what is often called the "national heritage." For example, early reaction to Europe's absolute monarchies along with a sense of freedom in this vast land resulted in a spirit favoring a republic and the separation of church and state. These are extolled. But often overlooked are facts like these: vast land holdings and distances contributed to justifications made by Christians for slavery! So rooted did this become that more than a century after slavery was officially abolished, racism lingers. Rugged individualism, necessitated

---

4. See Sydney E. Ahlstrom, *A Religious History of the American People* (Garden City, N.Y.: Doubleday, 1975), 1:200-470 and 2:79-358, for a comprehensive history of the churches in America.

first by settlement and then by expansionism into an untamed west contributed to a new type of classism, one that praised the successful and denigrated the hard-working poor. Westward expansions in the eighteenth and nineteenth centuries dislocated Christians. Denominational affiliations had already been dropped in many cases by the time of American independence. Many became unchurched. As the nation physically grew this only increased. The present unchurched factor in American religious life therefore has antecedents. Circuit-riding pastors and revivalism were the ways in which the churches responded in the last century. Crusades and other evangelical and pentecostal outreach programs are today's response. Electronic religious entrepreneurism, which combines fervor, financial sharpness, and technical know-how, stresses the successful individual and often advocates material well-being apart from God for some and because of God for others! In many cases it justifies certain political, social, and cultural stands that, when subject to the judgment of the gospel, are found lacking.

Rejection of institutional church affiliation, more common since the Second World War, accounts for today's large number of disaffected Christians. Correspondingly, a renewed sense of ethnicity has emerged with many Americans finding their sense of identity more and more in their roots. During the past four presidencies civil religion also has increased, offering Americans a substitute focus in which to place their trust and loyalty. Christopher Lasch, in *The Minimal Self*,[5] observes that they are not looking for life's meaning; rather, their all-absorbing quest is for survival. The threat of nuclear annihilation, always subtly if not blatantly present, undoubtedly caused this. This survival instinct has been stretched in meaning to refer not just to economic success but to prosperity. While this sometimes is the message of the so-called electronic church, it is more often the preaching of politicians who have become civil religion's icons of economic success by reason of their personal wealth. Civil religion, which is not to be confused with legitimate nationalism, is sometimes projected to such an extreme, as aspects of the Iran/Contra scan-

---

5. Christopher Lasch, *The Minimal Self: Psychic Survival in Troubled Times* (New York: W. W. Norton, 1985).

dal demonstrate, that it competes with one's sense of fidelity to God. Despite this, the American context still does excite faith and church affiliation. In the Western world there probably is not a more religious people from the point of view of church attendance and membership than the citizens of the U.S. Religious leaders address issues like the economy, nuclear warfare, and human rights—and are listened to. Citing biblical principles, religious groups (often ecumenical) effectively marshall protests against perceived evils and urge civil disobedience.[6] This quick overview raises an important point: what contributes positively to America's religious experience also negatively weakens it.

What are these factors? Four seem basic and embrace the others. This delineation is not arbitrary, nor is it an attempt to magnify or trivialize them, but to describe them summarily and within the limits of the shared insight of the members of our study group. They are enormously complex, and sometimes contradictory because of the professed concept of the separation of church and state. This doctrine stems from the abhorrence of the absolute monarchies from which Europeans sought to escape and the feelings of freedom they felt in this new land. Yet the consequences of this doctrine were different for African-Americans than for the purveyors of the contradictions. That is, political freedom and separation of church and state, while propagated for the benefit of some, were used by this same group to subjugate another group, blacks, who did not come from Europe. This fact alone accounts for what has been called "The American Dilemma" in which some are more equal than others. The Bill of Rights was made applicable to some in ways that excluded others. For these people, indeed for all American Christians, the issue should be, "How have the factors that have shaped American Christianity kept it from being worthy of the name Christian?"

The factors that have contributed the most, positively and negatively, to an American's religious experience are pluralism, liberty, individualism, and materialism.

---

6. For a discussion of religion and American public order see *Religion and American Public Life*, ed. Robin W. Lovin (New York: Paulist Press, 1986).

PLURALISM

America's glory is that it is a melting pot of nationalities form-
ing a great people. The idea of one nation under God so corre-
sponds to the Christian's appreciation of all humanity's ecumenical destiny in Christ (John 1:3-5, 12; Col. 1:15-20) that
America is sometimes exuberantly hailed as the new promised
land. There is a richness to the nation's ethnic multiplicity and
in the experience of many peoples living distinctly yet side by
side and as one. In part American pluralism came to be in reaction to post-Reformation European states. *Cuius regio, eius religio*
led to a structural centralization of society that reached right into
moral and philosophical ways of thinking. European whites left
this in order to construct a society that respected diverse structures, cultures, and ways of thinking, or simply to establish a
way of life that was not permitted in the land they left. Both were
achieved in America.

Or were they? The experience of many Americans of color
is that America is more a "stew pot" than a "melting pot" of
peoples. Some were incorporated into the U.S. because of acquisition or annexation of territories—Hispanics in the whole
southwest covering five extant states and Puerto Rico, and Native Peoples whose ancestral lands were taken and exchanged
for reservations. Others were "immigrants"—Asian Americans
(who often live in ghettos sometimes turned into tourist attrac-
tions, e.g., Chinatown) and blacks, for example. These people
do not and often have not been allowed to "melt"; not because
their human experiences are different, but because of the artifi-
cial barriers erected against easily identifiable groups. This
always placed them at the mercy of the dominant culture. Inte-
gration has usually meant assimilation. Many peoples, but especially African-Americans, have tried this approach and do not
like the consequences. The African-American and ethnic presence in religious pluralistic circles have never been fully understood or accepted by the wider society.

As it has developed, pluralism now requires respect for the
multiplicity of political views and secular philosophies that are
found within the United States as well as elsewhere. American
pluralism is a larger matter than simply religious pluralism. For

today's new immigrants, America is the land of political asy-
lum—the home of the free and the land of opportunity. Yet many
of these people face prejudice and economic classism. In American society many do not see this as a "religious" issue because
they would now posit a religious and secular duality in American life.

But others ask: What could be more religious than to work
for the eradication of social, economic, and political oppression?
What could be more religious than for oppressed persons to
present their needs before God in prayer? Who is to say that the
modern prophet for God is not the one who analyzes the social,
political, and economic context in order to provide the church
with an agenda to carry out its work of liberation? What could
be more religious than that? Yet within many churches this issue
is the cause of ideological and moral conflicts! Pluralism is both
the church's blessing and the reason for its many internal struggles. Undoubtedly it will continue to be so.

LIBERTY

Americans sing that the United States is the land of liberty, a nation loosed from the treatments of despotic government, the
place where one can live positively in the condition of freedom.
Americans believe that liberty is God's gift to humankind, given
to enable them to choose God and life. Liberty is the right to
make choices. Americans, with a legal constitutional guarantee,
may freely choose to practice a religion, to make political
choices, and to enjoy civil rights without constraint provided
they do not violate another's freedom. Stated theoretically, self-
determination rather than conformity by necessity is American
freedom. No one may impose a philosophy or way of thinking
on another. Freedom of speech and press practically guarantees
this. Freedom of religion is one of the best examples of it. Confessing faith itself is an exercise of American freedom.

Freedom in America has not always been universal. The nation existed for a lifetime before the constitutional guarantee of
freedom extended to all blacks. Today some speak of the
economic bondage of new immigrants, legal and illegal, and its

consequent denial of civil rights. So despite the law, some still do not enjoy the American ideal of freedom because other Americans prevent this. Others contend that because of affirmative action or compensatory justice *their* civil rights are being violated. One may have to agree legally that this is the case, but this aberration may be necessary in the light of the systematic exclusion of a group of people over many years from the freedoms that others have taken for granted.

For the majority of European-Americans, liberty is centered in relation to civil rights and governmental functions. There is a difference between the popular mindset of minorities and that of the majority group with regard to freedom and the role of government. Both majority and minorities in America would agree that the government and the church are mutually autonomous in matters of control each should have over the other. However, in order to safeguard the well-being of each person in society, the church, in the view of many minorities, is obligated to advocate for their case. This matter is crucial among oppressed peoples if they are going to confess the apostolic faith today.

On the other hand, many in the majority population have a utilitarian ethic that advocates achieving "the greatest good for the greatest number." Concomitantly they stress a laissez-faire governmental policy because it always works in favor of the utilitarian ethic. Lawmakers are usually voting the will of the majority. Nevertheless, it is equally true that many in the majority have joined with minorities in advocating justice and peace. They are the church in action, often up against other persons who feel that the business of the church is spiritual and not political! How can liberty for minorities and majority persons be maintained if confession of faith is merely to apply to the spiritual realm of life without agitation in the political realm by Christians? The same God whom we serve in the confines of the church and in our homes shows up in the political affairs of human beings as well.

Moreover, civil liberty for some means the total secularity of the state as well as the total separation of church and state. This implies for some that in America "one does not have to believe"! The separation of church and state, instead of promoting religious freedom so all might confess their faith(s) according to conscience, has sometimes promoted the exclusion of church from society. Public acknowledgment of religion is limited to the very least secularly acceptable common denominators. When church leaders like Catholic or Methodist bishops issue pastoral letters concerning economics and peace, those who adhere to the state's total secularity angrily denounce such involvement. Undoubtedly civil rights advocacy permits but also shapes how many Christians can confess their faith. The issue of freedom affects as much what is confessed as how it is confessed in word and deed. This is a most challenging aspect of the American context for confessing the apostolic faith today.

The secular American state has also been affected by committed Christians. The legal egalitarian outlook of Americans has been strengthened by those who engage with others in American society's self-corrective processes. Advocacy for the poor, deprived, and minorities represents this. In the larger world scene human rights generally are more discussed and given center stage. The churches in the U.S. have responded to these issues because of the gospel imperative (Matt. 25:34-45) to feed the hungry, give drink to the thirsty, clothe the naked, shelter the homeless, heal the sick, and visit the imprisoned. Americans are famous for their generosity and compassion. Most are aware of the blessedness of their land and their own human resources. Almost naturally they exhibit a willingness to share. Of course, the church people who display such concerns in overseas mission or in advocacy roles at home are sometimes resisted by government officials, or even by their own church brothers and sisters. Liberty does raise the issue of not only the "what" but also the "how" of confessing the apostolic faith.

INDIVIDUALISM

The individual in society is rightly understood to be the subject of liberty and its exercise, freedom. However, one does not mean this when speaking of individualism, which refers, rather, to that attitude of mind which sees opportunity available to anyone who will take it. Obviously it is related to liberty. Perhaps less obviously apparent is its relationship to the issue of the rights of women and other minorities in American society. Social stature is a key to appreciating this. Intrinsic to an American's self-esteem is his or her desire for achievement. Progress, any progress, is dependent on personal achievement, and therefore on opportunity.

The good effects of this are numerous. American inventiveness, creativity, and competitiveness have resulted in goods, services, and social conditions that have improved the quality of life. But individualism also has had other effects like the attitude that sees the individual as the center of all reality. Personalism is sometimes exaggerated. The stress on success has resulted in an individualism rightly described as "rugged." In the past, rugged individualism referred to the necessity of the often lone pioneer heading into and taming vast western spaces. Today it means "getting ahead," sometimes at any cost. One wonders if it is the cause of the so-called value vacuum in the lives of so many American youth? Ironically, the yearning for community runs deep in American society as well.

This is especially true of minorities whose mindset is one of group solidarity or corporate personality rather than individual freedom. Minorities have had to stress corporateness to effect those things the majority culture takes for granted as prerequisites for practicing individualism. Many have become inventive, creative, and competitive. Blacks in particular have had to stress corporate efforts so that those human rights, taken for granted by others, could be secured and insured. Regrettably, some blacks have abandoned corporate effort in favor of individualistic competition with other blacks in order to protect whatever upward mobility they have achieved. Just as the majority's individualism led to success at any cost, so the practice of blacks and others has degenerated into an individualism that has become destructive of community.

For many Americans individualism has had a religious effect because for them religion itself is personal and private! This is the dimension in which the government deals with religious questions. When one realizes that the more influential shapers of the United States and its Constitution, people like Franklin, Adams, Jefferson, and Madison, were deists enamored of Rousseau and the principles of the French Enlightenment, this is not surprising. For a faith like Christianity that by nature is communal, the privatization of its confession in American society is a distinct factor that cannot be avoided in the search for a current confession of the apostolic faith.[7]

MATERIALISM

The fruit of extreme individualism divorced from God is materialism. The United States took shape during the period when western Europe experienced a humanist revival called the Renaissance. The era proclaimed a creation-centered world. Although they professed religious faith, the first European-Americans actually saw their world as a vast, resource-filled, *earthly* symbol of bounty. The Horn of Plenty as an autumn and Thanksgiving symbol has more than decorative significance. In time, America became the land of opportunity for waves of immigrants and incorporated peoples. Consequently, they became pragmatists. Material gain became a value. Seen positively, materialism can be viewed as development, or humanity creatively controlling God's gifts to upbuild the human community and to foster human dignity (Gen. 1:28-31). Because of it Americans have been enabled to be one of the more generous peoples on this earth.

But American materialism has another side, consumerism. Consumerism is now so normal that it is considered a right. ("I want it all, and I want it now!") Many Americans are blinded to the exploitation of material and human resources within and beyond their borders so that this "right" can be preserved. Materialism combined with rugged individualism has led to the glorification of the entrepreneurship mentality whereby success is measured by the pursuit of status, the acquisition of wealth, and the wielding of power to protect what one has. These are things Jesus rejected (Matt. 4:1-11; Mark 1:13; Luke 4:1-13)!

Many of America's poor people, as they confess faith, ask how they can go beyond being mere consumers. How can they begin to take control of their own destiny through economic,

---

7. A recent study on the effect of individualism in American life is Robert Bellah et al., *Habits of the Heart* (New York: Harper & Row, 1985).

political, and social power (which it is hoped will be used for sharing and caring)? Their faith is confessed in this real-life context. After all, Jesus came to bring the "abundant life" that includes the total person. For two hundred years churches in America have proclaimed the gospel way of life. They still do. But the good in this society is constantly confronted by subtle, almost indiscernible forces that invert good American values. These have and will confront any lively and fruitful confession of the faith of Peter, Paul, and the apostolic church.

CONCLUSION

There is no easy description of the North American context. Added to what already has been observed one must include the current political situation in the U.S. and the nation's role in world politics. The multiplicity of churches with their diverse polities and particular traditions is also a factor raising another basic question: Can there be one, or must there be many accepted ways for Americans to confess the apostolic faith? Finally, due to the ecumenical, the feminist, the charismatic/pentecostal, and the evangelical movements one is led to recognize still another factor: the churches in America are at a changing point![8]

Noting this, the Christianity Today Institute met in January 1986 to focus attention on current critical factors influencing American religious life. The first is that the closing years of this twentieth century are undoubtedly the era of evangelical output, but of dubious impact. The impression is sometimes given, especially by the electronic church, that religion is preached merely to make Americans comfortable. Despite that, this is the era of heightened consciousness to the world's problems of hunger, injustice, and poverty. Today the church speaks for and stands with the powerless and the deprived. Never has the church been so "disestablishment." At the same time never has it been so establishment, mainline, traditional, or, if you prefer, fundamentalist!

---

8. *Changing Contexts of Our Faith*, ed. Letty M. Russell (Philadelphia: Fortress Press, 1985).

Three social realities seem to be changing churches in the U.S. Graphically put, congregations are getting older just as is the general population. Women are declaring their rightful place in the church at all levels, raising issues not even thought of fifty years ago. Churches are no longer white Anglo-Saxon Protestant and Irish or Southern European Catholic. Black churches have their own history and theology shaped by different influences than those of other churches. Many churches today are becoming significantly Hispanic. Orthodox Christians from Eastern Europe and the Eastern Mediterranean are the new Christian immigrants. Vietnamese and Korean congregations are springing up in mainline churches.

Across church lines several theologies are taught and stirring a neoconservatism. A new but undeclared ecumenism, it seems, is uniting evangelicals, traditional conservatives, and even the pope! All demand a return to fundamentals. Some associate the current search for spiritual experience with the desire for simple and absolute answers to complex issues. Never before in America have spirituality, retreats, and meditation been so much in the ascendency.

Finally, two other factors need notice. Denominational power has shifted, except perhaps in southern states where it is beginning to shift. Only two churches are significantly present throughout every state in the U.S., the United Methodist and the Roman Catholic. Most churches are regional if not outrightly local. Local churches are growing.[9] "Confessing the Apostolic Faith Today" in America is not only a struggle for a relevant creedal statement but one that preserves the united basis for a lived fidelity to the gospel in this complex context.

---

9. *Into the Next Century: Trends Facing the Church* (Carol Stream, Ill.: Christianity Today Institute, 1986).

APOSTOLICITY IN THE ROMAN CATHOLIC, EASTERN ORTHODOX, LUTHERAN, AND REFORMED TRADITIONS

JAMES JORGENSON

This chapter will highlight some of the commonalities and divergencies in the notion of apostolicity as understood and interpreted by the Roman Catholic, Eastern Orthodox, Lutheran, and Reformed churches. There are important similarities, but also significant differences that prevent full ecclesial unity between these churches.

What is the authentic apostolic faith was first addressed by Irenaeus of Lyons (ca. 190) in his *Adversus Haereses*. In several passages he demonstrates how the authentic apostolic faith may be distinguished from the "higher knowledge" asserted by the Gnostics:

> Anyone who wishes to discern the truth may see in every church in the whole world the apostolic tradition clear and manifest. We can enumerate those who were appointed as bishops in the churches by the apostles and their successors to our own day, who never knew and never taught anything resembling their [the Gnostics'] foolish doctrine. Had the apostles known any such mysteries, which they taught privately and sub rosa to the perfect, they would surely have entrusted this teaching to the men in whose charge they placed the churches. For they wished them to be without blame and reproach to whom they handed over their own position of authority. (3.3.1)

And again:

> Therefore it is incumbent to obey the presbyters who are in the church, those who as I have shown possess the succession from the apostles; those who, together with the succession of the episcopate, have received the certain gift of truth, according to the good pleasure of the Father. (4.26.2)

"Apostolic succession" primarily is understood here as fidelity to the apostolic proclamation and mission, and as continuity in the faith of the apostles. Correct doctrine and teaching are guaranteed by the uninterrupted successors of the apostles in the local community—the local bishop and the presbyters united with him. Apostolic succession is not so much the tactile transmission of sacramental powers as the transmission of truth, or of the faith received from the apostles. In Irenaeus' argumentation the obverse is clear: if the Gnostic fables were true, the apostles would have entrusted this teaching to their successors in whose charge they placed the churches.

For the Roman Catholic Church and the Eastern Orthodox Church apostolic succession is the orderly transmission and continuity of the teaching of the apostles, of ministry, and of sacraments throughout the centuries. This continuity and fidelity is signified, guaranteed, and effected by the successive ordination of bishops. In both the Latin and the Eastern traditions, at the ordination of bishops, the imposition of hands is preceded by an examination of and statement of faith by the ordinand. In the Roman Catholic Church apostolic faith is expressed by the church's teaching authority, or magisterium, the world's local bishops in communion with the bishop of Rome. The magisterium is ordinarily exercised by the pope and bishops teaching through pastoral letters, instructions, and exhortations. What is taught may be applied to particular circumstances, but it is the same faith of the ages taught by bishops everywhere. Extraordinarily but more manifestly, the magisterium is the world's bishops gathered and teaching through an ecumenical council. More rarely and in extraordinary circumstances Roman Catholics believe that the successor of Peter, the pope, may exercise the personal charism of infallibility by speaking *ex cathedra* on matters of faith and morals.

The Eastern Orthodox churches stress fidelity to the apostolic faith and its tradition and continuity similar to that of the Latin church. But in recent centuries its traditional ways of expressing faith have been severely challenged and new avenues are being explored that will be consistent with the great tradition. The form of the Petrine ministry—not papal primacy but universal jurisdiction and infallibility—constitutes a fundamental doctrinal and ecclesiological difference between these two ancient churches.

The magisterial Reformers of the sixteenth century— Lutherans and Reformed—intended to reestablish the fullness and purity of the apostolic faith after the perceived distortions and innovations in the life of the medieval Western church. In contrast to the Anabaptist Reformers who intended to reconstitute what they felt was completely lost, Luther and Calvin understood themselves to be in continuity with the past. They reformed and healed an ailing church not only by employing *sola scriptura*, but also by calling upon the practices and the writers of the early church to witness to their expressions of continuity in the apostolic faith. The recovery of the apostolic (scriptural) faith by the Lutherans and the Reformed was expressed through confessional statements. The Lutheran church is by definition a confessional church, the "Church of the Augsburg Confession." The content of the confessions is understood to be a correct interpretation of Scripture and therefore binding. The Lutheran Church–Missouri Synod is most affirmative about this. Since the Reformers felt they had recovered the apostolic and scriptural faith, the historic succession of the episcopacy was not considered essential to the nature of the church.

The Roman Catholic Church and the Eastern Orthodox Church maintain that councils accurately interpret the apostolic faith. While the content and formulation of council documents are never exhaustive, they nevertheless have permanent binding force. Councils, the consensus of the Fathers, and official liturgy *(lex orandi, lex credendi)* witness to the presence and guidance of the Spirit. The Roman Catholic, Eastern Orthodox, Lutheran, and Reformed traditions all hold to the conviction that councils/confessions authentically interpret and apply apostolic truth during time of doctrinal conflict. They may not and do not invent new doctrines. Philip Melanchthon remarked that the sign of the Holy Spirit's activity in the church is not that sin and heresy do not exist in the church, but that they can be detected and combatted.

To enable substantive progress in ecumenical theological dialogue and to determine the content of the apostolic faith, it is necessary to move beyond the dialectics of *sola scriptura* versus Scripture and Tradition. On the one hand, Protestant denominations as scriptural churches urging *sola scriptura* cannot agree on the content of scriptural apostolic faith. On the other hand, the ancient Latin and Eastern churches have disagreed over the development of doctrine and ecclesiology. Today the ancient churches do emphasize Scripture. And many "biblical" churches are recovering and reassigning value to tradition, as did the early Reformers.

The norm for church life and belief is fidelity to the teaching of Christ and his apostles. The earliest and most normative expression of this *Tradition* of fidelity is the New Testament. The Spirit continues to guide the church in fidelity to this teaching. All Christians are called upon to critique their life and beliefs in the light of the "apostolic faith" and the "faith of the church through the ages." Articulating the apostolic faith today depends on this perspective.

An exhaustive catalogue of the entire content of the apostolic faith is impossible. Its nucleus, however, is quite clear: belief in the triune God, the incarnation of the Son of God, his death and resurrection, and our salvation through faith in him. This is the principal content of the New Testament message and of Nicea's confession of the apostolic faith. On this virtually all Christian churches agree.

It seems appropriate to conclude by turning to Irenaeus and to his most succinct synopsis of the content of the faith of the church:

> The Church, although scattered over the whole world even to its extremities, received from the apostles and their disciples the faith in one God, the Father Almighty, Maker of heaven and earth, the seas and all that is in them, and in one Christ Jesus, the Son of God, who became incarnate for our salvation, and in the Holy Spirit, who by the prophets proclaimed the dispensation, the advent, the virgin birth, the passion and resurrection from the dead, the bodily ascension of the well-beloved Christ Jesus our Lord into heaven, and His parousia from the heavens in the glory of the Father to gather up all things in Himself and to raise the flesh of all mankind to life, in order that everything in heaven and in earth and under earth should bow the knee to Christ Jesus our Lord and God, our Savior and our King, according to the will of the invisible Father, and that every tongue should confess to

Him, and that He should pronounce a just judgment upon all and dismiss the spirits of wickedness and the angels who transgressed and became apostates, and the ungodly, unrighteous, lawless and profane, into everlasting fire, but in His graciousness should confer life and the reward of incorruption and eternal glory upon those who have kept His commandments and have abided in His love either from the beginning of their life or since their repentance.

This preaching and this faith the Church, although scattered over the whole world, diligently observes, as if it occupied but one house, and believes as if it had but one mind, and preaches and teaches as if it had but one mouth. And although there are many dialects in the world, the meaning of the tradition is one and the same. (*Adv. Haer.*, 1.10.1-2)

THE MEANING OF "APOSTOLIC FAITH" IN WORLD COUNCIL OF CHURCHES' DOCUMENTS

GEORGE VANDERVELDE

In the section on "Ministry," the Lima document on "Baptism, Eucharist and Ministry" deals with apostolicity in the context of succession in the apostolic tradition. Apostolic tradition in the church means "continuity in the permanent characteristics of the Church of the apostles." The following characteristics are mentioned:

> witness to the apostolic faith, proclamation and fresh interpretation of the Gospel, celebration of baptism and the eucharist, the transmission of ministerial responsibilities, communion in prayer, love, joy and suffering, service to the sick and the needy, unity among the local churches, and sharing the gifts which the Lord has given to each.[1]

Although the "apostolic faith" is considered one among many elements of the apostolic tradition, it plays a key role because it is presupposed in the other elements of the apostolic tradition. This foundational role is reflected in the basis of the WCC, which is described as "a fellowship of churches which confess the Lord Jesus Christ as God and Saviour according to the Scriptures and therefore seek to fulfill together their common calling to the glory of the one God, Father, Son and Holy Spirit."

Accordingly, the Edinburgh Conference on Faith and Order (1938), in a section on "Likeness of Faith or Confession as a Basis for Unity," speaks of "the revelation of God contained in the Holy Scriptures of the Old and New Testaments and summed up in Jesus Christ" as the "supreme standard of the faith." Further-

---

1. *Baptism, Eucharist and Ministry* (Geneva: World Council of Churches, 1982), Faith and Order Paper 111, par. 34.

more, it acknowledges the Apostles' and the Nicene-Constantin-opolitan creeds "as witnessing to and safeguarding that faith which is continually verified in the spiritual experience of the Church and its members."[2] The reference to spiritual experience makes clear that continuity in the apostolic faith is not a concern for the perpetuation of assent to a series of doctrinal statements in abstraction from daily life. This is underscored by the caution that the creeds are not to function as "legalistic standards."

The relation of the apostolic faith to the quest for the unity of the church was brought to the fore at the 1952 Conference on Faith and Order at Lund. A consensus statement on doctrine begins by affirming the normative nature of Scripture for doctrine, either as sole authority or as the primary and decisive part of authoritative sources. The ecumenical creeds are mentioned as interpretations or elaborations of the orthodox faith. The precise role of the creeds in maintaining the continuity of the apostolic faith is not clear, however.

In the same document the apostolic faith, centered on Jesus Christ, is directly linked to the unity of the church. The latter is approached, somewhat deductively, from Christology: "From the unity of Christ we seek to understand the unity of the church on earth."[3] This procedure presupposes a commonly accepted understanding of Jesus Christ and thus an acknowledgment of an "apostolic faith" in some form.

The Montreal Conference on Faith and Order (1963) dealt with the question of the apostolic faith under the theme, "Scripture, Tradition and traditions." This report distinguishes among "Tradition," "tradition," and "traditions." "By *the Tradition* is meant the Gospel itself, transmitted from generation to generation by the Church, Christ himself present in the life of the Church. By *tradition* is meant the traditionary process." The term *traditions* is used in order to refer to "the diversity of forms of expression" and the various confessional traditions.[4] The ques-

2. H.-G. Link, *The Apostolic Faith Today* (Geneva: World Council of Churches, 1985), p. 70.

3. Ibid., p. 76.

4. *The Fourth World Conference on Faith and Order* (Geneva: World Council of Churches, 1963), Faith and Order Paper 42, p. 50. Also Link, *Apostolic Faith Today*, p. 80.

22   GEORGE VANDERVELDE

tion of a criterion of authenticity and therefore of apostolicity is
raised in the context of the necessity of interpreting the tradition. But in the very formulation of an answer the original question returns: "Throughout the history of the Church the criterion has been sought in the Holy Scriptures rightly interpreted."
The next sentence poses the obvious question: "But what is
'right interpretation'?" A cerebral and legalistic notion of "apostolicity" is here avoided. By focusing on Tradition, described
ultimately as "Jesus Christ himself present in the life of the
church," the continuity intended by the "apostolic faith" is
centered on the living presence of Christ among his people.
Furthermore, the Montreal report avoids presenting apostolicity as an inert identity, but takes into account the widely varied
cultures within which the gospel is to resound as a "joyful, liberating and reconciling power."[5]

The report "Catholicity and Apostolicity" prepared by the
Joint Working Group between the Roman Catholic Church and
the World Council of Churches points out various aspects of
apostolicity, among which the following are the most important:

1. *Foundation:* The church is "built upon the foundation of the
   apostles (Apoc. 21:13 and Eph. 2:20)," and "its action is iden-
   tical with theirs."
2. *Continuity:* The Holy Spirit that the apostles received continues to act in the church and "their preaching is fixed in
   the New Testament writings which for this reason are called
   apostolic. The continuity of their witness and their action in
   the Church from the beginning is the work of the Holy Spirit
   and makes the Church apostolic."
3. *Variegated Task:* In view of the multifaceted tasks fulfilled by
   the apostles, the apostolicity of the church is credible only as
   it faithfully assumes "the tasks entrusted by the Lord to His
   apostles."
4. *Mission:* "It is . . . in virtue of its *participation in the mission* of
   Christ in the mission of disciples that the Church is apostolic.
   For the Holy Spirit manifests this mission, realizes it and
   communicates it in a community 'consecrated and sent' like
   Christ (cf. Jn. 17:18f.)."

5. *Fourth World Conference,* p. 59.

5. *Hope:* Because the kingdom is to be fully realized at the end of time, "apostolicity includes an intimate and essential link with the final accomplishment of God's saving plan.... This time of waiting for the return of the Lord is also for the Church the time of mission, for the dynamic presence of the Spirit, pledge of this living hope, makes the Church apostolic."

6. *Memory:* Because the apostles are agents in accomplishing the promises made to Abraham (cf. Heb. 12:1) and to the twelve tribes (cf. Matt. 19:28), the apostolic church "will also be catholic, necessarily, in space and time. Its memory embraces all the past which is constantly actualized in the Word and the Sacraments."

7. *Diversity of Ministries:* "The Church is apostolic because it continues faithfully, by the grace of God, the mission, the preaching and the ministry which it has received from the Apostles." The report notes that for some communions this entails the "apostolic succession."[6]

In an appendix on "Identity, Change and Norm," the Louvain report broaches the difficult question of continuity and identity with historical change. It affirms that "the identity of the Church in spite of and through all changes is to be found, basically, in the faith of its members, a faith which in all ages conforms to the unique and comprehensive truth of God in Jesus Christ." Because Christians may be mistaken in their understanding of the faith, however, the question of criteria and norm arises once again. The report points to the traditional norms for understanding the faith (Scripture, creed, the magisterium) but acknowledges that these themselves are subject to change. The norm is then identified as being the "universal saving truth of Jesus Christ, accessible to us in the apostolic writings." This is later identified as a subjective genitive: Christ himself is "the norm of the understanding of faith."[7]

Although the question of criteria for apostolicity is left unresolved, a new perspective is opened. The issue is approached

---

6. *Study Reports and Documents: Louvain* (Geneva: World Council of Churches, 1971), Faith and Order Paper 59, pp. 138-40.

7. Ibid., pp. 143-45.

dynamically by focusing on the living presence of Christ through the Spirit. This approach gives more room for the diverse manifestation of the church in various contexts. Whereas Lund employs a christological methodology, deducing the nature of unity from the nature of Christ, Louvain displays greater sensitivity to the historical, contextual diversity of the church. This is reflected by the way in which the Louvain report links apostolicity directly with catholicity. Similarly, a greater recognition of the pluriformity of the church is reflected in the understanding of the unity of the church in terms of a "conciliar fellowship," which was introduced by the Uppsala assembly, developed at the Salamanca consultation, and adopted by the Nairobi Assembly (1975) and again by the Vancouver Assembly.

Two further elaborations concerning apostolicity need to be considered. First, at a consultation in Rome in 1983 a "preliminary working definition" of the term was presented. It deserves to be quoted in full:

> The term "apostolic faith" as used in this study does not refer only to a single fixed formula or a specific moment in Christian history. It points to the dynamic, historical *(geschichtliche)* reality of the central affirmations of the Christian faith which are *grounded* in the witness of the people of the Old Testament and the normative testimony of those who preached Jesus in the earliest days ("apostles") and of their community, as attested in the New Testament. These central affirmations were further *developed* in the Church of the first centuries. This apostolic faith is expressed in various ways, i.e. in individual and common confessions of Christians, in preaching and sacraments, in formalized and received credal statements, in decisions of councils and in confessional texts. Ongoing theological explication aims at clarifying this faith as a service to the confessing community. Having its centre in the confession of Jesus as Christ and of the triune God, this apostolic faith is to be ever confessed anew and interpreted in the context of changing times and places in continuity with the original witness of the apostolic community and with the faithful explication of that witness throughout the centuries.[8]

Although the notion of apostolicity is presented here as a dynamic and multifaceted category, a specific historical starting

---

8. Link, *Apostolic Faith Today*, p. 266.

point is given. The Lima document "Towards the Common Expression of the Apostolic Faith Today" (1982) singles out the Nicene-Constantinopolitan creed as the foundational document that gives expression to the apostolic faith:

> A primary assumption of this project is the recognition of the Nicene Creed. For, together with a growing convergence in our understanding of baptism, eucharist and ministry, the appeal for a common expression of the apostolic faith belongs to the movement towards the unity of the Church. In the attempt to work out such a common expression, it is impossible to disregard the special place of the Nicene Creed. It is the one common creed which is most universally accepted as the formulation of the apostolic faith by churches in all parts of the world, where it primarily serves as the confession of faith in the eucharistic liturgy.[9]

In sum, the following aspects of apostolicity come to the fore in the WCC documents:

1. The identity of the church depends on its continuity with the apostolic tradition.
2. Within the multifaceted apostolic tradition, the apostolic faith is foundational for the identity of the church.
3. Apostolicity is a dynamic reality, consisting in the presence of Christ as confessed by his followers.
4. Unity in the apostolic faith exists in the pluriformity of Christian traditions in a great diversity of contexts.
5. In the quest for the common expression of the apostolic faith, the churches are asked to recognize the Nicene-Constantinopolitan creed as the ecumenical symbol (i.e., confessional document) *par excellence*.
6. The fundamental criterion *(norma normans)* of apostolicity lies in the consonance of our faith "with the testimony of the apostles to God's revelation in Jesus Christ" as recorded in the Scriptures.

---

9. Link, *Apostolic Faith Today*, pp. 216-17.

REFLECTIONS ON APOSTOLICITY IN THE NORTH AMERICAN CONTEXT

Donald W. Dayton

Since the emerging convergence around the "Baptism, Eucharist and Ministry" document of the Faith and Order Commission of the World Council of Churches, attention has to some extent moved to the struggle of the churches to find a common "confession" of the apostolic faith. As this has happened, it has become increasingly apparent that the North American context has distinctive elements that recast questions of apostolicity and the issues of "confessing the apostolic faith today." Several aspects of the American context deserve special notice.

The European discussion, it seems, has been dominated by the "ancient churches," especially by the Roman Catholic and the family of Eastern Orthodox churches, and by the churches of the magisterial Reformation, that is, the Anglican, Reformed, and Lutheran families of churches. For a variety of reasons— like the period of settlement by Europeans, the haven North America provided for various dissenting traditions, and the cultural freedom that provided the space for the emergence of new religious styles—church life in North America in many ways has been dominated by styles of religious life quite different from those of Europe.

While most of the European Christian traditions are present in the North American context, in some cases the translation has required adjustments. Even though the Roman Catholic Church is clearly the largest Christian denomination, the Protestant experience for much of the life of the United States has been the dominant cultural and religious force. But within the Protestant context the mix is quite variable. The classical Protestant traditions were especially influential in the colonial period. Puritanism held sway in New England. The Baptists and Quakers were in leadership in Rhode Island and Pennsylvania respectively. Various other Reformed traditions predominated in the middle colonies. Anglicanism's chief influence was in the South. But during the early national period it was Methodism, transplanted from England where it was an influential but still culturally marginal movement, that proved to be a dominant Protestant force. During the settlement of the midwest it became the largest Protestant body and helped to set the tone for many of the rest of the Christian denominations. Simultaneously, the Baptists began to grow, especially in the South—and the broader revivalist culture began to produce new variations such as the "Disciples" or Campbellite tradition.

The experience of slavery brought to North America a sizeable black population that suffered alienation and marginalization because of racism even after emancipation. Nevertheless it found expression in the distinctive experience of the black church, living chiefly within the Baptist, Methodist, and pentecostal traditions. The nineteenth century was especially fertile in new church formation. Not only were there new religious movements such as Mormonism on the fringes of the classical Christian tradition but there were also new denominations more closely related to the tradition. These included on the more conservative side the Seventh-day Adventist and Advent Christian families, and on the more radical side the Jehovah's Witnesses and other like groups. Another whole family of churches were produced by the mid-nineteenth-century holiness revival. In addition, a variety of "restorationist" traditions came into being. At the end of the nineteenth century the family of pentecostal churches emerged from a radical wing of the holiness movement.

Such dynamics and new movements have produced an extremely complex and diverse ecclesiastical situation in the North American context—one that is somewhat distanced from the European context as well as from the styles and ethos of the classical Christian traditions. Because of the influence of Anglo-American mission movements in the nineteenth and twentieth centuries in various parts of the world, this complexity has been exported to other areas of the globe where the newer American churches have been among the most productive evangelistically.

Consequently, Latin American Protestantism is dominated in many cases by the holiness and pentecostal churches. The North American experience not only provides a rich resource for exploration in and of itself, but also has global and ecumenical implications as a bridge between the European context and the situation in other parts of the world.

When we turn our attention to a closer analysis of the North American scene itself, the situation appears more complex than even the above analysis would suggest. Under the influence of recent discussions of contextualization, we had expected to find distinctive themes reflected in American church life, but we were not prepared for the extent to which churches found themselves related in diverse ways to that culture. The discovery of this diversity was a helpful reminder of the complexity of "contextualization." The following are some of the ways in which the North American churches understood themselves to be related to their context:

1. For many of the classical churches the North American experience has been one of adaptation to a new environment. For some churches this has been a movement from establishment to disestablishment (Roman Catholic, Eastern Orthodox, Anglican, etc.); for others this has been experienced primarily in terms of the nature of the ethnic or immigrant experience (Mennonites, Reformed Church in America, etc.). These factors have led to several levels of readjustment from the more practical and immediate (e.g., questions of language for worship) to the more theological (the "Americanist" controversies and issues).

2. For some churches with origins elsewhere this problem has been made especially acute by the fact that their churches have found the North American context the place of their major growth and influence—so much so that the American church is now the "mother church" shaping the life of the rest of the family. This is true for the Church of the Brethren and probably for Methodism.

3. Some churches think of themselves as shapers of American culture. This is especially true of the larger churches that have had major cultural impact. The United Church of Christ, presumably reflecting primarily its Puritan experience, considers itself in this light. But other groups, especially Metho-

dists, Baptists, and various other Reformed traditions, could as well.

4. Still others think of themselves as influenced by the American ethos or by currents that have had special force in this context—either more broadly in the sense of such themes as "individualism" or more specifically by such movements as "revivalism" or "fundamentalism."

5. This question is made especially acute for some churches because they are American products in a more direct sense. They were born on this continent. These include the various Campbellite or "restorationist" traditions including the Church of God, the holiness and pentecostal clusters of churches in their many and diverse variations, Adventist churches, and the various black churches.

6. A number of churches, especially those with a high "countercultural" commitment like the peace churches, are inclined to speak of their relationship to North American culture in negative terms. Their primary task has been to witness against tendencies of the North American experience (materialism, individualism, militarism, etc.).

7. Some churches, particularly the black churches but other minority and class-based churches as well, have been even more alienated from the dominant culture—even more than have the countercultural churches. Their relationship to the American experience is profoundly ambivalent and needs to be understood dialectically.

The complex American church scene, with its diverse patterns of adaptation that came about because of an unusual degree of freedom of expression and experimentation with new forms of cultural and religious life, must be taken into account in any analysis of the meaning of *apostolicity*. Each of these facets of experience reflects the vision of being apostolic and gives it a different nuance. Each of these traditions, and each of these experiences, brings a new angle of vision to the discussion. This complexity is given a new context when one realizes that the American scene has given a special dimension to issues of apostolicity. In order to be faithful to the truth *the North American church experience has struggled very intensely with questions of discontinuity and continuity.*

Even the more established traditions of American church life, for example, the Puritan and Congregational traditions of colonial New England, were very conscious of separation from the "Old World" and the effort to found a new order in the "New World." The rise of "revivalism" in the nineteenth century brought an emphasis on "restoration" and the "revival" of something that had been lost. This frequently took the shape of a search for the "revival" of an "apostolic faith" that had been lost. One is struck with the range of new meanings given to "apostolic faith" in the American context. Even Walter Rauschenbusch, the most prominent founder of the social gospel tradition, sought the emergence of a new "apostolic era." At the same time the protofundamentalists were appealing to "apostolic doctrine" to support their dispensational premillennial eschatology that led them out of the social gospel. The nineteenth century was filled with "restorationist" movements driven by a certain ecumenical vision to transcend the patterns of denominationalism. By founding various Churches of God they claimed to find this unity in the reestablishment of some feature or another of apostolic doctrine and practice. One might argue that this impulse culminated in the pentecostal tradition at the turn of this century. The pentecostal movement self-consciously called itself *the* "Apostolic Faith" because of its claimed restoration of the supernatural gifts of the New Testament church. A radical wing of the movement has since preempted the label "Apostolic Faith" to protest against the dominant trinitarian theology of Christianity. It claims to "restore" the faith of the apostles before the doctrinal consensus of the church councils.

This complexity is given further impulse by the fact that many American churches derive from the Free Church experience, or have had to adapt this to the American style. This means that many American churches carry in their memories, often subliminally, certain fears and concerns about their experience with the classical traditions. This in part accounts for a certain "anticreedal" tendency in some American churches. They associate creeds with moments of oppression that drove them to this "New World." Since the Methodist experience many churches have been inclined to assert continuity with the apostolic age along lines other than creedal, such as piety, ethics, and church structure. Some of these do not think of the "apostolic faith" as something to be "confessed" in creeds or even expressed propositionally.

These distinctive features of the North American church's complexity make any discussion of apostolicity difficult to comprehend and organize. But, at the same time, one must admit its richness, which has the possibility of expanding our horizons and deepening our perceptions of Christian faith. As a result, efforts to bring some coherence to the discussion have not been entirely satisfactory. Our study group's discussions produced at least two different ways of organizing the materials that were collected from representatives of the various churches.

A. The first typology addresses the three basic ways of conceiving "apostolicity":

1. *Tradition:* This emphasizes continuity in ministry, sacraments, and perhaps teaching with the apostles. We think of this approach primarily in relation to the ancient churches, especially the Roman Catholic, Orthodox, and Anglican. This has sometimes been expressed mechanically because of the concern for an unbroken line of sucession, or more loosely in terms of "being in fellowship with the apostles." It places a premium on issues of ecclesiology, especially ministry and sacraments.

2. *Teaching:* This mode emphasizes continuity in terms of doctrine and teaching and is characteristic of the magisterial Reformation churches, especially the Lutheran and Reformed. They broke lines of succession but needed nonetheless to demonstrate continuity along the lines of preserving the "truth" or the "teaching" of the apostles. These churches have specialized in writing "confessions" incarnating apostolic "truth," utilizing "faith" as the organizing principle.

3. *Praxis:* This emphasizes continuity in terms of some understanding of ethics or practice that has continuity with apostolic practice and is characteristic of churches of the radical reformation, Methodism, and various other restorationist movements born out of the American experience. These churches often have been nontraditional in ecclesiology and have not specialized in the doctrinal articulations of faith. They more likely have left behind organizations for social relief (e.g.,

the Mennonite Central Committee, the Friends Service Committee, and campaigns for abolition, relief of the poor, etc.). This cluster of churches is very complex and could be said to organize their understanding of Christian faith around the theme of love rather than faith—or at least to see the latter as instrumental to the former.

This typology has several advantages. It draws explicit attention to the newer churches. They are not well understood within the ecumenical movement, which appears dominated by the concerns of the older churches and those of the magisterial Reformation. Although there is a certain chronological validity to this typology and although it highlights some significant issues, it also seems to be too clear and simple, obscuring the complexity of the American experience. Another typology might better become the organizing principle for understanding the complex American context for confessing the apostolic faith.

B. The second typology contrasts the historical (and developmental) and restorationalist (or primitivist) modes of understanding continuity with the "apostolic faith." Within each of these there are different axes of continuity (church life, teaching, practice, etc.).

The first would comprise those traditions that emphasize historical continuity and/or succession as the basic mode of conceiving of apostolicity. They allow in many cases for an understanding of doctrinal development. For them the usual pattern of continuity is sacramental. Forms of ministry ensure the preservation of the integrity of the life of the church and its teaching. But one can see something like this in other traditions as well. The report of the Southern Baptist experience mentions the movement of "Landmarkism" and its claim to an unbroken succession of "baptist" churches back to Christ or to John the Baptist. Parallels undoubtedly exist in other traditions, too. Witness, for example, the tendency of some pentecostals to find a similar unbroken chain of the practice of the charismatic gifts that cuts across traditional church lines.

The second would comprise traditions that accept a breaking of the historical link to the apostolic church but insist upon the possibility of a "restoration" of the apostolic faith. These churches accept another kind of development in the church (that which is seen as inappropriate—or as a "fall") but have a tendency toward forms of biblicism and primitivism that do not easily accommodate doctrinal development in the ordinary sense. These traditions find the point of contact with the "apostolic faith" along different and, at times, contradictory lines such as the following:

1. Finding continuity in forms of church practice (orders of ministry, structures of governance, use or nonuse of musical instruments). Many Baptists could fit this pattern.
2. Emphasizing continuity of teaching or doctrine. The churches of the magisterial Reformation come to mind.
3. Emphasizing the restoration of a lost form of piety or spiritual vitality. Methodism could be seen here because Wesley affirmed a Constantinian fall of the church—similar to the radicals—but primarily along the line of piety rather than church/state relationships. Many of the "revival" traditions would fit this pattern, especially Pentecostalism with its emphasis on the restoration of the "apostolic faith" in terms of miracles (healing, etc.) and charismatic gifts.
4. Finding continuity in the teaching and guidance of ethics and/or life-style that may or may not overlap the categories of church practice and piety. The historic peace churches seem to illustrate the tendency of a cluster of churches to see apostolicity primarily in terms of life rather than doctrine. The Southern Baptist claim to "restore" the "Great Commission" and the practice of evangelism seem to fit here, too.

This second typology elevates issues that are lost in the earlier one and reveals more clearly some of the ways in which traditions cross the lines of the other typology. It also specifies in more detail the variety of modes of apostolicity that are too easily grouped under the third category of praxis in the first typology. But either of these ways of organizing the materials collected indicates the range of perceptions of what it is to be "apostolic." Therefore any articulation of the "apostolic faith" has to take into account the various dimensions of Christian existence and experience that both of the above typologies raise.

APOSTOLICITY AND ORTHOCHRISTIANITY*

*Church of God (Anderson, Indiana)—Methodists—Quakers—
Baptists—Mennonites*

DEAN FREIDAY

The ecclesial communities or families listed above in reverse
order of founding have little in common at first glance. They
range in size from the Baptists (25.5 million in the U.S. with 14
million Southern Baptists alone—the largest single Protestant
denomination) and the Methodists/Wesleyans (13 million with
9.5 million in the United Methodist Church) to whole families
measured only in thousands (Quakers 110, Church of God 184,
Mennonites 288).[1]

Large or small, these families originated or rediscovered important dimensions of apostolicity and have had genetic effects
on numerous other communities. Methodism alone gave birth
to the African Methodist Episcopal, African Methodist Episcopal Zion, and Christian Methodist Episcopal churches (four million combined), the Salvation Army, and the Wesleyan Church.
Methodists also inspired the holiness movement that further developed into Pentecostalism (probably ten million more not
under the Methodist banner).

Even the Quakers, smallest of all, did their share of siring
and cross-pollenizing. Hannah Whitall Smith, a Philadelphia
Quaker, played a major role in the holiness movement's found-

---

* Note: Throughout this paper and notes, italics have been added by
the author, with the single exception of the quoted portion of the Lord's
Prayer in the section on the Methodists, in which the italics appeared in
the original.

1. World Almanac, 1985, pp. 356-57 (from the 1984 *Yearbook of American and Canadian Churches*).

ing and wrote its lasting spiritual classic, *The Christian's Secret of a Happy Life* (1875). Wesley's doctrine of perfection owes some original shaping to Quakerism.[2] And there was a Quaker Methodist Connexion in England for some time. High-church Anglican William Law (1686–1761), who produced *A Serious Call to a Devout and Holy Life*, probably of "more influence than any other post-Reformation spiritual book except *The Pilgrim's Progress*,"[3] was influenced by Quakers and in turn influenced John Wesley.

The author of *Pilgrim's Progress* was, of course, the Independent John Bunyan. A Baptist, Benjamin Keach (1640–1704), reintroduced hymn singing to British Protestantism. William Carey (1761–1834) formed the Baptist Missionary Society, becoming missionary to India in 1793 and initiating "the modern movement of the missionary expansion among Protestant churches."[4] The "social gospel" of German Baptist Walter Rauschenbusch (1861–1918) brought about social involvement in the U.S. by many Protestant groups (the Methodist Social Creed of 1908 is recited in some places as often as the Apostles' Creed!). E. Glenn Hinson's three-volume *Doubleday Devotional Classics* (1978) drew the attention of many Protestants to spirituality. He also edits *The Baptist Peacemaker*, which was launched in 1980 and almost overnight had a circulation of forty thousand.

It is easy to dismiss smaller churches as irrelevant if one is infected with the "major denominations" syndrome.[5] Even the

---

2. Cf. Dean Freiday, "About the Apology," in *Barclay's Apology in Modern English*, ed. D. Freiday (1967; rpt., Philadelphia: Friends Book Store, 1980), pp. xxiii, xxxv.

3. *Oxford Dictionary of the Christian Church*, 2d ed., rev. by F. L. Cross and E. A. Livingstone (London: Oxford University Press, 1974), s.v. "Wm. Law," p. 805.

4. Roman Catholics, of course, had long been active in the mission field. Not only did the gospel spread throughout the Roman empire in apostolic times, but the Jesuits—in particular— were indefatigable. They had been to India and China and much of Latin America by the middle of the sixteenth century. Moravians were the first Protestants, as early as the 1730s, to engage in missionary activity.

5. "There is a great danger in the way the World Council of Churches is going. Ecumenical services are a jolly good idea, and churches coming together is a very good idea, but I don't think that the practices of the

smallest groups are not immune to claiming triumphally the pos-
session of "true Christianity." Perhaps their real contribution is a
reminder that the Nicene Creed's "marks of the Church," as
Avery Dulles, SJ, has pointed out, were originally interpreted
qualitatively.[6] Each of our churches helped broaden the definition
of OrthoChristianity by a particular emphasis: on works (ortho-
praxis) for some; on some aspect of experience (orthopeira)—
holiness, sanctification, or perfection—for others; on a prophet-
ic/mystical relationship to God (orthopresence) for still others;
and on the right ordering (orthotaxis) of both church and society
for others. In spite of this "specialization," initially at least, they
all were aware that unless these claims are based in Christ as Lord
they deteriorate into utopian ideals or pragmatic goals. Methodism affirms that efforts "to speak to the human issues in the
contemporary world" must be prayerful and thoughtful and
stem "from a sound biblical and theological foundation."[7]

> Estranged from God, men and women wound themselves and
> one another and wreak havoc throughout the natural order.
> Human hopes for achieving the good are thwarted as long as we
> seek to realize such ends apart from God.... [Yet] God's unfail-
> ing grace shows itself in his suffering love working for our re-
> demption.[8]

It is also significant for our churches that "the community
that receives the most severe reprimand" in the Book of Revelation "is not accused of any particular grave fault" nor of being
unorthodox as Pergamum and Ephesus were, but of being

---

largest of the Western churches should be taken as the standard for every-
body else." John Punshon, tutor in Quaker Studies at Woodbrooke Col-
lege, Birmingham, England, in an interview in *Quaker Life* (Richmond,
Ind.), June 1986, p. 24.

6. Avery Dulles says, "There was little basis in Scripture or in the
early tradition for understanding unity, holiness, catholicity, and apostolicity as the visible marks of an organized society." *Models of the Church*
(Garden City, N.Y.: Doubleday, 1974), p. 134. And, "In the community
model of the Church, the notes are no longer interpreted as the visible
marks of a given society, but rather as *qualities of a living community*" (pp.
135-136).

7. *The Book of Discipline of the United Methodist Church—1984* (Nashville: United Methodist Publishing House, 1984), p. 86.

8. Ibid., p. 74.

neither cold nor hot.[9] Lukewarmness has probably been the church's most frequent shortcoming, something these renewal movements addressed themselves to along with other highly significant matters—sometimes for the first time, sometimes for a second or third time. This chapter's purpose is to depict the living witness of these communities in a way that may offer an example—or sometimes a warning—to other ecclesial communities.

ORTHOPRAXIS ON CHRIST'S MODEL— THE ANABAPTISTS/MENNONITES

Walter Klaassen turns Luther's dismissal of Anabaptism as "a revival of monasticism" and "righteousness by works"[10] into a constructive framework for situating both Mennonites and other restoration and renewal movements. "Anabaptists were by no means the first to break with old forms and develop new ones, or to level basic and incisive criticism against the Church." "Monasticism provided for repeated breakthroughs to renewal" and initially protested "against the development of a double standard of morality" in which "only the clergy and some other select persons could live out the teachings of Jesus" considered "too demanding for the common people." At first individual lay men and women sought renewal through faithfulness—especially through the profession of the "evangelical counsels" of poverty, chastity, and obedience—but also to Jesus' other ethical imperatives. Individually, and later in communities, they attempted to call the church "back to the demands and promises of Jesus." Out of Klaassen's development of monasticism's contribution, only St. Francis of Assisi can be given space here. He, more than any other saint, has captured the imagination of Christians other than Roman Catholics. In his own day he was so popular that he founded a lay person's order for those who

9. Jean-Louis D'Aragon, SJ, "The Apocalypse," 64:30 in *The Jerome Biblical Commentary*, ed. Raymond E. Brown, Joseph A. Fitzmeyer, and Raymond E. Murphy (Englewood Cliffs, N.J.: Prentice-Hall, 1968).
10. Walter Klaassen, *Anabaptism: Neither Catholic nor Protestant* (Waterloo, Ont.: Conrad Press, 1973), p. 28.

wished to follow a rule of life based on "true faith and conversion of heart" in the circumstances of everyday living. "The
Franciscan movement in the thirteenth century," Klaassen says,
"espoused the simple following of Jesus as the heart of Christian obedience."[11] Interestingly, William J. Whalen remarks of
John Wesley that "had he been a Catholic instead of an Anglican, he probably would have launched a revival . . . [like
St. Francis] or perhaps . . . founded a religious order."[12] Similarly, Robert Barclay (1648–1690) says that among Quakers there
were many in whom God had so

> effectively produced a mortification and abstraction from the
> love and pursuits of this world . . . [that] even though they have
> daily commerce with the world, are married, and lawfully em-
> ployed, this redemption has been as complete as that which used
> to be considered possible only for those who were cloistered or
> in monasteries.[13]

A former Roman Catholic priest, Menno Simons (1496–1561),
so successfully organized the loosely knit groups of Anabaptists
into a family that they now bear his name. He wrote that "obedience is one of the 'marks of the church,'"[14] and affirmed that

> *Obedience to Christ*, the Lord, is an *integral part* of faith. And faith
> then is confidence in the certainty of God's love and Grace as
> shown in Jesus, and includes *following Him* . . . the evidence that
> confidence is genuine. Christ is Lord not only because salvation
> is available through Him alone, but also because He becomes the
> One who determines what a man *is* and *does* as the model and
> example of a God-pleasing life. . . . "Whosoever boasts that he is
> a Christian, the same must walk as Christ walked."[15]

Mennonites were well aware that the school of Christ is "the
School of Tribulation."[16] Both Mennonites and Quakers criti-
cized Luther for so emphasizing "faith" as the key to salvation
that "it made no demands upon anyone" and was "misleading

---

11. Klaassen, *Anabaptism*, p. 28.
12. William J. Whalen, *The Methodists* (Chicago: Claretian Publications, 1967), p. 7.
13. *Barclay's Apology in Modern English*, p. 394.
14. Klaassen, *Anabaptism*, p. 25 (from CW, p. 740).
15. Ibid., p. 20 (the concluding internal quotation is from CW, p. 255).
16. Ibid., p. 21, from Hans Hut.

and abstract." Anabaptists regarded Christ as the center and norm of Scripture. While they would not have ascribed an equal or superior value to the Bible as a written text, they would not have found it inconsistent to call it "God's word" in a secondary or derived sense. For the Anabaptists "the life and teachings of Jesus and the Apostles—in their actual, simple, clear words— was the luminous source and fountain of truth. Everything else was secondary and would have to be judged by it."[17] The reference to actual, clear words represented a conviction that by multiple-sense exegesis the "simplicity and directness of the Gospel had been hopelessly compromised."[18].

"Disciplined, sharing, and witnessing congregations"[19] were the primary context within which, or at least in close relation to which, exegesis needed to be done. "The gathered disciple community . . . [seeks], where possible, a common understanding" of Scripture's intent.[20] Like Roman Catholics, Mennonites "insisted that works were important and . . . could not be separated from faith." "Faith if it is genuine will be expressed in *action* that agrees with confession."[21] Where Luther established "the Gospel" as opposed to "Law" as the canon within the Canon for interpreting Scripture, Anabaptists saw that *Christ was not only the Measure* of what constituted "divine revelation," but also was determinative of *the kind of authority* that different books and particular texts were to have. Anabaptists did not establish levels of bibilical authority through systems of propositions analogous to conciliar decrees. Neither did they oppose "revelation" to "propositions." Most Anabaptists sought to discern levels of biblical authority by working from within the Scriptures rather than by imposing criteria from outside. Pilgram Marpeck (d. 1556) was especially

> insistent that any theological claims must be christologically based. For God's revelation in Christ represents the limits of what we know. . . . What goes beyond Scripture proceeds not from revelation but from reason. . . . Theological knowledge is

17. Klaassen, *Anabaptism*, p. 42.
18. Ibid., p. 41.
19. Ibid., passim.
20. Ibid., p. 80.
21. Ibid., pp. 77-78.

always fragmentary. . . . [Attempts] to fill the gap by reason ought to be abandoned as dangerous.[22]

COVENANTING TOGETHER TO WALK IN GOD'S WAYS—THE BAPTISTS

There has been much confusion about the relationship of the Baptists and Anabaptists largely because Baptists in England were called Anabaptists to discredit them. Except for a single congregation in exile in Amsterdam, Baptist beginnings were entirely in England. Anabaptist groups originated in several continental countries. John Smyth (ca. 1554–1612), a Separatist from the Church of England, had some contact with Mennonites in Amsterdam and adopted their "believer baptism," but coupled it with Arminian rejection of predestination. The year he died, some members of his congregation returned to England and constituted a church under the pastorate of Thomas Helwys (ca. 1550–ca. 1616). This became the nucleus of the General Baptists (so called for their polity, allied with that of the Presbyterians).

How far was the English Baptist movement as a whole influenced by the continental Baptists? A Baptist theologian, Robert C. Walton, says:

There are some striking resemblances. Both movements have the same negative characteristics, the spirit of criticism and of disappointment that the Reformation did not immediately achieve a a perfect Kingdom of heaven upon earth. Both rejected the State Church and demanded full liberty to worship God as the Spirit directed them. Positively, both emphasized the "holy community" of which the symbol was Believers' Baptism, and sought to live by the ethics of the Sermon on the Mount, and to resist the pressure of the secular world. Both used a simple Scriptural form of worship. But there were striking differences also. The English Baptists never refused the obligations of citizenship. They were not pacifists. They were willing to take the oath and to enter public service and they obeyed the civil power so long as it did not seek to control the life of the Church. They were not markedly millenarian, and they did not accept suffering and injustice

---

22. Klaassen, *Anabaptism*, pp. 43-44.

meekly as their share in the Cross of Christ. Rather, they engaged
in political activity, joined the New Model Army, and fought in
Civil War. The roots of the English Baptist Movement lie in English Puritanism and Separatism. It was altogether too English
. . . to owe its inspiration and forms . . . to the Continental sects.[23]

The other principal early Baptist group, the Particular Baptists, was established in Southwark in 1633 and developed into
associations rather than into the "connections" of the General
Baptists. Their theology was Calvinist (including predestination). Both spread through lay evangelists and New Model
Army soldiers.[24] Two smaller groups originated in the seven-
teenth century. The Seventh Day Baptists wedded Saturday Sab-
batarianism to apocalyptic expectations. Fairly numerous in
Colonial America, only five thousand members remain today in
sixty-three congregations. The other group was not so much an
"organization" as a "cross section of the General and Particular
Baptists" who were willing to fraternize, "especially with Independent Paedobaptists" later known as Congregationalists.[25]

Like most Separatists from the religion established by law
under the Elizabethan Settlement, Baptists were imprisoned.
Under Charles II their worship was made illegal. Particular Baptists shared little except for Calvin's theology about the "National Church," which was "Erastian in church order and government and largely medieval in liturgy."[26] They sought to be a
"true visible Church" of people "separated from all knowne
syn." They were gathered inwardly by "the Spirit, Faith and
Love," and outwardly by "a vow, promise, oath or covenant
betwixt God and the saints." To gather, "they joined hands . . .
stood in a Ringwise . . . made some confession or Profession of
their Faith and Repentance. . . . Then they Covenanted together
to walk in all God's Ways."[27]

In spite of the Baptist emphasis today on immersion, it was
not required until 1644 by the Particular Baptists, and not until

---

23. Robert C. Walton, *The Gathered Community* (London: Carey Press,
1946), p. 63.
24. Ibid., p. 69.
25. Ibid., p. 71.
26. Ibid., p. 59.
27. Ibid., pp. 81-82.

1660 by the General Baptists.[28] For both *transformation* was the inward work of Christ with the "laver of regeneration."[29] In spite of subsequent professionalization

> the distinction between clergy and laity is foreign to the early Baptist tradition. . . . The Pastoral Elder might be a working man, a farm laborer, a tailor, a shoemaker, a tinker; but God had called him, and the church had trained him in the things of the Spirit. He was gifted, he was faithful, and his motives were pure.[30]

As these Baptists understood it, the gathered church was probably nearest to the order found in the New Testament. Christians were

> called out to this present evil world, to live in a new and holier fellowship. . . . *To be heretical about Church Order* was, to them, as perilous to the soul as to be *heretical about a statement in the Apostles' Creed*. To countenance any other form of the Church than the Holy Community was not simply to be unscriptural, it was to put one's . . . salvation in jeopardy.[31]

To Baptists, itinerant evangelists or "messengers" were not ministers of local congregations. These "home missionaries," to use a later terminology, were supplemented by missions abroad in the late eighteenth century. Baptists became "one of the largest Protestant and Free Church communions" with a world membership in 1968 of "probably thirty million" and a "community strength" of ninety million. In the U.S., in addition to the large American Baptist Convention and the fourteen million Southern Baptists, there are over eight million Black Baptists in two additional conventions. German, Swedish, French, Hungarian, Danish, Italian, Finnish, Norwegian, Polish, Rumanian, Mexican, and Czech ethnic expressions can also be found. Strongly Calvinist "hard shell" Baptists, denominationally Primitive Baptists, offset the strongly anti-Calvinist Free Will Baptists whose slogan is "free grace, free will, and free salvation." With such diversity it is difficult to delineate overall characteristics.

---

28. Walton, *Gathered Community*, p. 82.
29. Ibid., p. 86.
30. Ibid., p. 102.
31. Ibid., pp. 93, 104-5.

ORTHOPRESENCE AND ORTHOTAXIS— THE QUAKERS

Like Anabaptists, early Quakers insisted they were neither Catholic nor Protestant because, in their view, both were radically in error. Neither the first Reformation of Jan Hus (ca. 1372–1415), the magisterial Reformation of Luther and Calvin, nor even the radical Reformation of Anabaptists and others had gone far enough. These "Reformers" merely lopped off some unhealthy branches. George Fox (1624–1691) uprooted the whole tree and began Christianity again.[32] For Fox apostasy started in the apostles' days and has continued ever since. *Restorationism* is the word used in connection with those communities that saw the restoration of apostolic simplicity as important. The early Friends, however, did not ape every practice found in the New Testament. They were not primitivists.

Restoration meant proclaiming "the everlasting Gospel again." They took the command to preach from Revelation 14:6 rather than the so-called Great Commission in Matthew 28:19 with its suspect trinitarian formulation.[33] They did so probably to add an eschatological context and to wed "realizable eschatology" to a new understanding of the role of Christ. The central christological image for Friends was Christ as Prophet—not a reduction to a mere prophet, but a development of the Son, Savior, and Lord in the role of Teacher by his living presence. Their whole concept of "communion" and community was built around his being "in the midst of them" (Matt. 18:20), a text often limited to eucharistic presence. Christ's presence was particularly important to the Quaker understanding of the Gathered Community. Theirs was no *voluntary association* as in some Protestant doctrine. They were a people *called into being* by their living Lord. Christ was present in all his offices and functions, but pri-

---

32. Cf. Henry J. Cadbury, *Quakerism and Early Christianity*, 1957 Swarthmore Lecture (London: George Allen & Unwin, 1957).

33. "This formula is probably a reflection of the liturgical usage established later in the primitive community. It will be remembered that Acts speaks of baptising 'in the name of Jesus.' See Acts 1:5f. The attachment of the baptised person to all three persons of the Trinity will have been made explicit only later" (note on Matt. 28:19 in the New Jerusalem Bible).

marily as the Prophet "who had come to teach his people himself." It was a "second coming" in the Spirit like the New Testament apparitions that did not rule out the final coming in judgment. Every aspect of both community and individual life stemmed from Christ's prophetic role. Although John Calvin had developed his Christology around Christ as Prophet, Priest, and King he gave no content to the title "Prophet." For Fox, however, "Prophet" was cardinal and indispensable even though it was only one of the more than fifty christological images he employed. A "Valiant Sixty" of itinerant evangelists proclaimed "the everlasting Gospel" in marketplaces, open fields, jails— wherever Providence placed them. Or they challenged the National Church in the open period in worship provided by law.

The itinerant preaching of Fox and others led to "settled meetings" (particular churches) when there were enough adherents in a particular area. Here no emphasis was given to sermons or to any prearranged service. Worshipers simply waited in silence for the Spirit of Christ to minister as needed. Sometimes the Spirit would prompt vocal utterances where appropriate, or heal spiritually, sometimes physically, through repentance and self-conviction. Or the Spirit would renew those who despaired or suffered, or would sanctify by disclosing the way to reconciliation with God and one's fellows. The Friends felt called both to proclaim and to demonstrate that Christ had indeed inaugurated the reign of God on the earth. Whoever spoke in the context of faith did so *not* because he or she had been appointed by the congregation but because Christ "ordained" on the spot, and revealed his holy will to them. There was no "setting apart"; that they evidently spoke for Christ, and were equipped by grace, alone counted. Although Friends did not "prooftext," their preaching was a veritable catena of Bible phrases or passages with an occasional citation of a palmary text. In their business sessions as well, Friends were not governed by earthly power or considerations of earthly authority. A clerk's "presiding" was limited to maintaining an agenda and minuting "the sense of the meeting" that had been arrived at by the subordination of each person to Christ and following his model of humility and patience.

Friends were reluctant to structure permanently even acts of compassion or social justice. Activities in certain fields were channeled and perpetuated by the gradual development of "Testimonies"—prison reform growing out of their own seventeenth-century imprisonments; oaths proscribed because of Christ's own unqualified command (Matt. 5:33-37; see also James 5:12). Friends gave women an equal role from the start and took steps toward the elimination of slavery. It was abolished in Pennsylvania and New Jersey among themselves in 1776 and shortly afterward among Friends elsewhere. They have consistently worked toward ending violence and war by substituting an international rule of law and equity.

The insistence that Revelation continues (in the sense of *new applicational insights, not new doctrine*), combined with their reluctance to fix patterns and structures, probably accounts in part for the numerous social reforms credited to Friends.[34] "Gospel Order" (*orthotaxis*) was understood by Friends for the world as well as for the church. The kingdom of God could be entered and lived in, however imperfectly, in this age. God would reign in all fullness when God willed. Meanwhile God calls us to cooperate in opening the Way under the direction of Christ by applying the relational models of compassionate love that Christ offers, by joining him willingly in suffering on behalf of the dispossessed, and by witnessing to his own manner of life and ministry. According to Quakers those who do so will prob-

---

34. Women's accomplishments alone are outstanding: Margaret Fell (1614-1702), the "mother of the faith" to all Quakerism was a Parliamentary lobbyist and a good theologian; Elizabeth Fry (1780-1845), whose prison work among women in England matched the international work of the evangelical Fellow of the Royal Society, John Howard (1726?-1790) who spent £30,000 of his own money; Betsy Ross (1752-1836), the creator of the American flag; Susan B. Anthony (1820-1906) and Lucretia Mott (1793-1880) both of whom worked for women's suffrage. Lucretia Mott also labored for the abolition of slavery. In the twentieth century Quakers have produced (among others) Emily Balch, the second woman to receive the Nobel Peace Prize (Jane Adams was first); Elizabeth Grey Vining, who tutored the Crown Prince of Japan; Mary Calderone, a medical doctor who at the age of seventy decided to become an expert on sexuality; Dame Kathleen Lonsdale (crystallographer and physicist), who was one of the first two women to be admitted to The Royal Society. A list of male social achievers would be equally impressive.

ably find salvation in their faithfulness and become Christ's brothers and sisters and children of the One heavenly Father in the process.

ORTHOPEIRA (ORTHOEXPERIENCE)— THE METHODISTS

There were two major formative influences on John Wesley—a little society for the perfection of holiness at Oxford University and a worship service at a Moravian church in Aldersgate, London. The Oxford society began simply in 1727 when his brother Charles persuaded two or three others to meet "first every Sunday evening, then two evenings a week, and finally every evening from six until nine o'clock."[35] Upon his return to Oxford John Wesley "immediately associated himself" with the group and "was recognized as its head." The society combined study of the classics and the Bible in Hebrew and Greek with visiting prisoners, the poor, and the sick.

The Aldersgate *religious experience, a conversion"* took place when John Wesley, newly returned from his first pastorate in Georgia, was convinced that his twenty months there had been a fiasco both with his congregation and his mission to the Indians. He had said to himself that he "who went to America to convert the Indians" had not yet been "converted to God." Wesley had met Moravians on shipboard and been impressed with their imperturbability during a stormy trip. With some reluctance he went to the Aldersgate meeting where he not only felt his "heart strangely warmed" but *assurance* that Christ had taken away his sins. After Aldersgate he proposed "to promote as far as I am able *vital practical religion.*"[36] Anglican pulpits had already been closed to him, but at age thirty-five he, his brother Charles, and George Whitefield began to preach to the common people wherever they could be found. John himself preached an average of three times a day for more than fifty years (42,400 ser-

---

35. Charles Claude Selecman, *The Methodist Primer* (Nashville: Methodist Evangelistic Materials, n.d.), p. 11.

36. Ibid., pp. 13-14, and *O.D.C.C.*, s.v. "John Wesley," p. 1467.

mons) traveling 250,000 miles by horseback. In spite of his Oxford education and broad scholarship in Christian literature of all periods, his preaching was simple and no one ever "observed in him the affectation of learning." He simply urged following Christ in a surrender that leads to *transformation of life,* and proclaimed the joy and peace that "flow from fellowship with Christ and his people."[37]

John Wesley "bequeathed to Methodism the idea that the gift of Christian perfection is *both an event and a development,* both an offer of *an immediate experience* and an *ever-growing sanctification* of the whole of life. Both process and crisis have a place."[38] Methodism continues to believe that the church's mission is "to spread scriptural *holiness* and to *transform* all peoples and all nations through the gospel of Christ."[39] Although Methodism affirms the ancient creeds and confessions as "valid summaries of Christian truth," it does not "invest them with final authority" or "set them apart as absolute standards." Nor does it accept "the 'confessional principle'—the claim that the essence of Christian truth can, and ought to be, stated in precisely defined propositions legally enforceable by ecclesiastical authority."[40] Early in its history it developed a dictum: "As to all opinions which *do not strike at the root of Christianity,* we think and let think."[41] And "to this day *conduct* rather than *creed* is the test of membership."[42]

Anglicanism, rather than the continental Reformation, provided most of the original doctrine for Methodism. The situation in the U.S. has had a formative influence as well. Under frontier influence "it was the *Wesleyan hymnody* that served as the most important single *means of communicating* the doctrinal substance of the gospel and in its guardianship as well."[43] By

---

37. *Primer,* pp. 34-35.

38. Claude H. Thompson, "Wesley's 'Doctrine of Christian Perfection'" in *We Believe: Twelve Articles on Methodist Beliefs* (Nashville: Abingdon, 1962), p. 70.

39. *Book of Discipline,* p. 10.

40. Ibid., p. 41.

41. Ibid., p. 40.

42. *Primer,* p. 18.

43. *Book of Discipline,* pp. 45, 48, 49.

uniting in 1968 with the Evangelical United Brethren Church the United Methodist Church has acquired some of the "mellowed Calvinism of the Heidelberg Catechism" and Article XVII from the Lutheran Augsburg Confession about the last judgment. Both are interpreted in a typically nondogmatic temper.

"No motif in the Wesleyan tradition has been more constant or insistent than the linkage between Christian doctrine and Christian ethics."[44] In spite of the lament that action does not always match intention, the Methodist involvement in social issues is substantial. And the only official affirmation of faith that American Methodism as a whole has produced is the Social Creed of 1908.[45] While retaining this creed, which was largely influenced by Baptist Walter Rauschenbusch's social gospel, a new and enlarged statement of Social Principles was adopted by the General Conference of the United Methodist Church in 1972 and revised in 1976.

ORTHOPRAXIS AND "OPEN MEMBERSHIP"— CHURCH OF GOD (ANDERSON, INDIANA)

As with the other churches treated here, a protest against current Christian practice was involved in the founding of the Church of God. Building on Methodist foundations in many ways, and believing that a church is apostolic to the degree that it conforms to the New Testament church, the Church of God endeavored to get back to the simple teachings and practice recorded in Scripture. Daniel S. Warner (1842–1895), who initiated the movement through publication and itinerant evangelizing, considered "sectism" then to be the culprit. Today we would be more likely to fault *institutionalism* rather than *"sectarian confusion."*[46]

As Warner outlined it in 1887,[47] he embarked on a nonsectari-

---

44. *Book of Discipline*, p. 50.

45. Interview with Marjorie Suchocki.

46. John W. V. Smith, *The Quest for Holiness and Unity: A Centennial History of the Church of God* (Anderson, Ind.: Warner, 1980), p. 445. Until his death several years ago, John Smith had served as a member of the Faith and Order Commission of the NCCC for many years.

47. Ibid., p. 443.

an movement. Wesley andthe founders of the Disciples of Christ, Thomas Campbell (1763–1854) and his son Alexander Campbell (1788–1866), had hoped that their movements would unify Christians. In each case there was a gradual evolution. In the Church of God they hoped that all the holy would "join in one great fellowship open to all the redeemed."[48] The apocalyptic battle had been joined on "separation from sin and sectism."[49] Warner and his associates "were not anarchists," but advocated "divine organization." For a century they struggled "to know and implement government by the Holy Spirit" and were unwilling to use "any of the three standard formulas for Church polity—episcopal, presbyterian, or congregational—[but lacking an] overall system . . . [there] has been a somewhat unconscious utilization of all three" for parts of the polity that did evolve.[50]

In 1880 there were no local pastors, only "flying messengers."[51] What little coordination and centralization the beginning movement had was provided by the Gospel Trumpet Publishing Company. It resembled a monastic community where each worker "agreed to give his complete labor to the publishing work in exchange for only food and clothing. All income was reinvested in the work, and any partner or his heirs could draw out only what that member had originally invested without interest."[52] By the time *The Gospel Trumpet* had made its fifth move, to Anderson, Indiana, in 1909, the work had grown so that a hotel-like facility to house "200 volunteer workers" was needed. Changes had to be made, however, as congregations grew. Changes were also made "to reconcile the paradox of an unorganizable church being organized to accomplish goals,"[53] and a shift from largely rural to urban and suburban membership.[54] The church has been interracial from the beginning, with its national agency staff 14 percent black by 1963.[55]

---

48. Smith, *Quest for Holiness and Unity*, p. 437.
49. Ibid., p. 200.
50. Ibid., p. 437.
51. Ibid., passim.
52. Loc. cit.
53. Ibid., p. 318.
54. Ibid., p. 207.
55. Ibid., p. 385.

The Book of Acts is very important to Church of God members, not in the sense of their trying to mimic first-century church life but in their intention to live in continuity with the spiritual character of the church as it is portrayed in Acts. One way of describing this character of the church of apostolic faith, using Acts as the biblical touchstone, is as follows:

1. It is a truly ecumenical community of believers that is devoted (a) to the study of the apostles' teaching; (b) to the interpersonal experience of being common participants in a new divine reality; (c) to the breaking of bread for both physical and spiritual nourishment; and (d) to earnest prayer (see Acts 2:42 and 4:31). Furthermore, miraculous occurrences announce the inbreaking of the new era of God's reign. Mutual help, support, and sharing within the community are the order of the day. Gladness, praise, and joy are predominant traits of the community, even in times of extreme trial (see especially the account of Paul and Silas in Acts 16:22-25).

2. Conversion to *both* Christ and his church is normative, as is seen in Acts: "and there were added that day about three thousand souls" (2:41); "And the Lord added to their number day by day those who were being saved" (2:47); and "The number of the disciples multiplied greatly in Jerusalem" (6:7). In Acts, people are converted to Christ and to his church simultaneously. Conversion to Christ in isolation from his ecumenical community is not in the apostolic tradition.

3. Worship leads to evangelism and evangelism leads to worship. The upward and inward experience in worship is based on the backward and forward relatedness to God's action in history, and leads to the downward and outward movement of service to human need and evangelism to the ends of the earth. But the goal has not been reached when persons are converted. The goal of evangelism is that the converted might be brought into the fellowship of divine worship, beginning here and now to participate with the universal congregation of believers both on earth and in heaven as they praise and adore the triune God.

4. Holy Spirit baptism is the power for the entire sanctification of the believer's life so that nothing whatsoever is able to turn him or her away from devotion to the Lord.

5. The church of apostolic faith is made orderly so that the

divine mission can be accomplished with the greatest degree of effectiveness. Acts gives evidence of (a) orderliness in personal lives, a negative example being that of Ananias and Sapphira (Acts 5:1-10); (b) orderliness in congregational life (Acts 6:1-7, and the Council at Jerusalem, "minutes" of which are found in Acts 15); and (c) orderliness in the missionary endeavors of the church (Acts 1:8 giving the plan of action: "in Jerusalem and in all Judea and Samaria and to the end of the earth"). This orderly pattern becomes the plan for the church's expansion as it is set forth in Acts.

6. The pentecostal effusion grants communication of and participation in the gospel, and thereby builds up the community of gospel faith. The obliteration of the barriers of gender and age were heralded in Peter's Pentecost sermon when he quoted from Joel (see Acts 2:17-19). Also, the barriers of language were broken down on the Day of Pentecost (Acts 2:1-12) and the barrier of nationalism was dealt with in Peter's vision prior to the conversion of Cornelius. In the church of apostolic faith, the Spirit's upbuilding of the church means the breaking down of barriers to gospel communications and community; furthermore, whenever there is an unwillingness for the Spirit to break down barriers, the upbuilding of the body of Christ is greatly inhibited.

7. Apostolic faith is guaranteed only through the vertical working of the Spirit, which must be always in harmony with the Christ present in the New Testament. The Spirit works with persons in all ages and places, leading them to faithful response to the biblical gospel, bringing them to trust in Christ for salvation, moving them to confess the faith as set forth in Scripture, and inspiring them to live in loving obedience to the Lord of the church.

Traditions of the apostolic faith do not guarantee the *reality* of apostolic faith; only the *God* of apostolic faith can do that. The God of apostolic faith can and does initiate new expressions of the faith that are not necessarily in horizontal continuity with the postbiblical traditions of the faith, but which are, nevertheless, in vertical, faithful continuity with the biblical traditions itself.

The relationship "between *sound doctrine* and *authentic expe-*

rience"[56] had become crucial and continues to be a major question. Keeping "open membership" for all whose hearts and minds are "turned toward Christ," and maintaining a noncreedal stance requires a delicate balance. The seminary faculty celebrated the movement's centennial by working through to a carefully considered *We Believe* statement[57] that contains a series of mutually agreed affirmations of faith stated in very fresh and positive terms.

The message of churches like these is that apostolicity is not simply orthodoxy in isolation, but includes Christ's *reciprocity factor:* "Whatever *you did* for one of the least of these . . ." (Matt. 25:40, NIV) or "if *you forgive*" (Matt. 6:14, NIV). Since the time of St. Francis of Assisi (d. 1226) little and large movements have repeatedly emphasized the importance of *practice* and living like Christ. *Orthopeira,* authentic experience, has been the dimension of apostolicity to come to the fore most recently. Two members of our group—the Church of God and the Quakers—have insisted on *orthotaxis. Orthopeira* has been raised in the church with many voices—medieval mysticism, ascetical and sanctifying practices, the holiness movement, and, in our own time, Pentecostalism. The Holy Spirit will continue to move whomever, wherever, and whenever the Spirit wills. At times when the winds of the Spirit assume gale force the church can only "hold on to the handlebars" and ride out the storm. Thanks and praise be to God: *Veni Creator Spiritus!*

---

56. Smith, *Quest for Holiness and Unity,* p. 425.

57. *We Believe: A Statement of Conviction on the Occasion of the Centennial of the Church of God Reformation Movement,* by the faculty and staff of the Anderson School of Theology (Anderson, Ind.: Warner, 1980).

THE APOSTOLIC FAITH IN THE AFRICAN METHODIST EPISCOPAL ZION CHURCH, ASSEMBLIES OF GOD, THE EPISCOPAL CHURCH, AND THE UNITED CHURCH OF CHRIST

CLYDE STECKEL

The task of describing the apostolic faith in four quite diverse traditions like the African Methodist Episcopal Zion Church, the Assemblies of God, the Episcopal Church, and the United Church of Christ may seem less taxing than the attempt to state commonalities and differences, but there are formidable obstacles in the way of an accurate accounting. Lack of detailed knowledge is an obvious barrier. The failure to grasp subtle nuances of meaning and language will mar the results. Differing sympathies color the descriptions, however irenic in spirit and ecumenical in commitment they may be. And the question of topics is always there. Is it more "apostolic" to begin with the oldest tradition and move to the youngest? Or does one begin with the tradition judged to be most fully apostolic? The assumption here is that all are apostolic, each in its own way. Therefore the presentations will proceed *alphabetically!*

THE AFRICAN METHODIST EPISCOPAL ZION CHURCH

The AME Zion Church, like other black denominations in America, came into existence out of the history of black slavery and discrimination. Emerging out of the Wesleyan tradition, the AME Zion Church shares with other members of that family the

53

episcopal order, the Wesley version of the Anglican Articles of Religion, the use of the Apostles' Creed in worship and instruction, and a connectional church system.

This church understands missionary work to be a fundamental mark of its own apostolic character. Jesus Christ is the one who calls and commissions the church to its mission. He is the norm of that mission. And he is the head of the body, the church. Christ's mission is one of proclaiming the good news of freedom, of God's justice, and the call to end every form of oppression and inequality. The AME Zion Church affirms other Christian traditions as sharing the apostolic faith so long as they reject any white supremacist or other racist doctrines in their teachings and practices. Once that fundamental inclusion is assured, other matters can be negotiated, including pulpit and altar fellowship among local churches of differing denominational traditions.

What stands out for the AME Zion Church is the christological shape of the apostolic faith. Jesus Christ calls the church to mission and to justice; he calls the church into being and is head of the body. Creedal, liturgical, and ecclesial definitions are grounded in that christological foundation and are always tested by that center. It is, to be sure, unlikely that traditional Wesleyan features of this church could be easily changed. But its strong commitments to freedom and justice for black people will continue to have the effect of keeping concerns about a classic definition of the apostolic faith off center stage.

ASSEMBLIES OF GOD, PENTECOSTAL

The Assemblies of God comprise a grouping of pentecostal communities that established a General Council in 1914 and have continued to maintain a denominational self-identity since that time in the midst of a larger number of pentecostal communities around the world. While agreeing to be a "noncreedal" church, the General Council of the Assemblies has understood itself to be in fellowship with the larger church and in agreement with many doctrines held by other conservative Christian bodies in America. These doctrines are summarized in sixteen "fundamental truths," adopted by the General Council in 1916. In 1969 the General Council adopted a statement to guide its recognition of the apostolic faith in other bodies, including the inspiration of Scripture, the divinity of Christ, and other "cardinal teachings" (undefined) essential to biblical Christianity.

But these creedlike statements do not quite express the heart of the pentecostal tradition. A personal experience of accepting Jesus Christ as personal Savior and receiving Spirit baptism are central to the life of these churches. While strong emphasis has been placed on the gift of tongues as decisive evidence of a true Spirit baptism, other gifts are counted as well. Spirit baptism is not used as a criterion to determine whether other Christians are within the apostolic fold. But the Assemblies do believe that all Christian bodies would more fully reflect continuity with the apostolic tradition if Spirit baptism were practiced more widely.

As the Assemblies of God reflect on their partnership with others in the effort to restate the apostolic faith for today, at least two main issues claim the attention of the partners: (1) Are non-pentecostal churches open to a fresh emphasis on the Holy Spirit and its gifts? And in return will the pentecostals be open to a variety of Spirit theologies and Spirit expressions? (2) How far will the doctrinal formulations of the Assemblies, reflecting both their early twentieth-century vocabulary and their common ground with other evangelicals, be open to the thinking and language from other theological traditions as the apostolic inquiry proceeds?

THE EPISCOPAL CHURCH

The Episcopal Church, as part of the worldwide Anglican Communion, recognizes the scriptural witness as the basic norm of faith, employing a critical interpretive method. In addition to the biblical norm, tradition and reason are criteria for testing the apostolicity of doctrine. The Episcopal Church has a strong sense of being in direct continuity with the apostolic faith of orthodox Christianity, though at the same time reluctant to define faith too narrowly or be quick to detect heresy. The doctrine of the incarnation and the liturgical expression of the faith are very much at the heart of the Episcopal tradition. The Nicene Creed continues to be its eucharistic creed. The Catechism, the Eighth Article of Religion, and the 1979 Prayer Book all affirm the Apostles' and Nicene Creeds as statements of basic belief.

The Lambeth Quadrilateral Bishops' Statement (1887) on reunion with other communions identified the Bible, the two creeds, baptism and eucharist, and the historical episcopacy as the basis for reunion. While the historical episcopate is not viewed as essential to the being of the church, the Episcopal Church does believe that the well-being of the church is enhanced by it. Therefore, other communions lacking the historical episcopacy are invited to be open to its benefits. Similarly the Episcopal Church invites other bodies that confess Jesus Christ, but are not ordered sacramentally, to give fresh consideration to baptism and the eucharist.

The Episcopal Church perceives itself as well positioned to continue its mediating and integrating vocation among the Catholic, Orthodox, and Protestant traditions. But the social and cultural heritage of the historic Church of England suggests that a different set of "ecumenical" issues will be faced in the quest for a shared apostolic faith tradition, issues raised by the church's political establishment in England, upper socioeconomic identification in the United States, and the colonial heritage it signals in Africa and Asia.

THE UNITED CHURCH OF CHRIST

In 1957 the United Church of Christ was formed by the Congregational-Christian churches and the Evangelical and Reformed Church. The process of combining Reformed, Lutheran, Puritan, and revivalist traditions, along with presbyterial and congregational polities, has required patient and persistent organizational and educational effort. The Reformed emphasis on faithfulness in public and social transformation has been an important motif in this new church, along with an ecclesial emphasis on the fullness of the church in each local congregation, grounded in the Word and guided by the Spirit.

In 1962 the UCC adopted a new statement of faith for use in

worship and instruction, but not as a test of orthodoxy. The historical drama of salvation in Jesus Christ is a central theme in the statement, along with emphasis on the discipleship of the Christian community and its members. Theological critics have questioned its adequacy in stating clearly the nature and interrelationship of the persons of the Trinity, but for the most part the UCC seems to have found it to be both expressive of its faith and formative of Christian identity where it is used.

Some congregations of the United Church of Christ also use the Apostles' Creed in worship. And some (a smaller number) employ the Nicene Creed in their eucharistic liturgies. While the Constitution of the UCC affirms that its faith is grounded in the creeds of the ancient ecumenical councils, it would be difficult to document how actively these creeds function in the preaching, teaching, and worship of the UCC.

It is clear, however, that in both its theory and practice the UCC affirms that Jesus Christ is the head of the church, head both of the whole church and of each local church. Denominational structures are important for the well-being of the whole church, but they have no ultimate authority over the local church. It is more likely to be in discussions of polity and decisions about action on moral and social issues that the liveliest UCC theological formation takes place. As a participant in ecumenical efforts to explore the meaning of the apostolic faith for today, the UCC is more likely to focus on "life and work" issues than on "faith and order." Here it may find itself on more common ground with the AME Zion missionary emphasis than with a stronger creedal emphasis as in some other churches. The experience of Jesus Christ and a Spirit baptism in the Assemblies of God would strike a resonant spiritual chord in many UCC churches, though the forms of expression would differ. And the Episcopal emphasis on faith taking shape liturgically rather than propositionally would be shared in many UCC churches.

Each of these four traditions expresses its apostolic character in significant measure by reference to Christology. This is schematically and summarily expressed:

AME Zion	Jesus Christ is the one who calls to mission for justice.
Assemblies of God	Jesus Christ is personal Savior, opening the way for Spirit baptism.
Episcopal Church	Jesus Christ is experienced liturgically and sacramentally.
UCC	Jesus Christ is head of the church, locally as well as globally.

These differing christological accents need not be contradictory or exclusive, but are mutually enriching. This shared christological focus also suggests that each tradition might be challenged to develop more fully its thinking about God as Creator and Sustainer of the universe, not apart from the history of salvation centered in Jesus Christ but in ways that will deepen and clarify the meaning of that history in relation to other cultures and religious traditions.

Conclusion:

DIMENSIONS OF THE APOSTOLIC FAITH

The Faith and Order Commission's apostolic faith substudy group for recognizing apostolicity pursued its inquiry by attempting first to discern what criteria are employed by member traditions of the Christian family in North America to maintain their own apostolic fidelity and to recognize that fidelity in other members of the family. Although it was exceedingly fruitful, in the end it seems best to speak of *dimensions* of apostolic faith, not criteria. Passing judgment on the faithfulness of other traditions as the word *criteria* suggests seems premature. Since this study's aim was mutual understanding and discernment, its findings are presented in a spirit of growing mutual understanding. They are organized descriptively, not normatively. We hope the day is not far off when member traditions in the Christian family can engage one another in fashioning normative agreements about the apostolic faith. To that end we dedicate this summary and offer some suggested next steps.

THREE DIMENSIONS OF APOSTOLIC FAITHFULNESS

Three dimensions of apostolic faithfulness emerged in our study as organizing categories:

1. *Dimensions shared, however differently, by all members of the Christian family.* These are: confessing Jesus Christ as God and Savior; the guidance and inspiration of the Holy Spirit; the authoritative witness of the Scriptures; the church as the community of faithful worship, witness, and service in the world.

2. *Dimensions shared by some member traditions of the Christian family, but not by others.* These are: normative creedal and confessional statements; normative episcopal and teaching offices; normative polities; normative experiences of conversion, sanctification, holiness, and liberation.

3. *Dimensions of apostolic faithfulness that reflect the historical and cultural matrix* in which a particular church tradition has come to expression. These, however, are not viewed as normative by other traditions. Historically these have been called *adiaphora*, or matters of "indifference" when it comes to defining the necessary elements of faith. These dimensions are nevertheless vitally important for understanding the rich diversity of Christian life and expression. In ecumenical dialogue they become pathways to deepened understanding and occasions of gratitude for God's gifts. This study did not attempt to record or analyze all those diverse Christian expressions where we are mutually tolerant and seek to increase mutual understanding. Rather the focus is on those dimensions of apostolicity that are shared by all traditions and on those shared by some traditions but not by others (paragraphs 1 and 2 above). The rest of this presentation considers only these two.

1. Dimensions Shared by All Members of the Christian Family

A. *The Confession that Jesus Christ is God and Savior*

The traditions represented in this Apostolic Faith Study share the following ecumenical expression of the apostolic faith that is contained in the "Basis of the World Council of Churches"; they "confess the Lord Jesus Christ as God and Saviour . . . according to the scriptures . . . and seek to fulfill their common calling to the glory of the one God, Father, Son and Holy Spirit."

This compact group of phrases points to the central incarnational claim shared by all the traditions. The *exposition* of this confession, however, illustrates their diversity. They range from simple baptismal formulas to elaborations in creedal and confessional statements that are understood to be regulative of the faith of the community. Two historic expressions of this confession are of particular note: the Protestant Reformation's, especially Luther's emphasis on the radically free gift of God's grace in Jesus Christ as Lord, Savior, and Teacher; and the holiness and sanctificationist traditions that insist that works of love and righteousness, performed as disciples of Jesus, constitute a truer test of this confession than any particular verbal formulation.

B. The Guidance and Inspiration of the Holy Spirit

These appear in the formal creedal and confessional statements of many Christian bodies. They come to particular focus in the eucharist, in the other sacraments, and in preaching where it is understood that the gift of the Spirit guides both the speaker and the hearers. But there are also "Spirit traditions" and "Spirit movements" in the Christian family that affirm the radical "breaking in" of the Holy Spirit. This is represented by particular Spirit gifts, including the gift of a regenerate life, of tongues, and of healing. Even though these Spirit churches may not formally insist on particular gifts of the Spirit as normative for apostolic faith, the experience of the Spirit is profoundly formative in their worship and beliefs, making it difficult for them to feel at home with Christian groups where the Spirit is experienced more formally. Other Christians may fear that an undue reliance on the Holy Spirit opens the door to private interpretations (and the doubtful belief and actions arising therefrom) that are difficult to justify through references to Scripture and/or tradition.

C. The Authoritative Witness of the Scriptures

The primary place of scriptural witness represents a growing ecumenical consensus in the late twentieth century. There seems to be more and more agreement that historical-critical interpretive methods must be employed if the scriptural voices are to speak clearly and authoritatively to our own time. Nevertheless, significantly large groups in the Christian family continue to insist that the texts of Scripture are essentially self-interpreting and literally mean what they say as directly inspired words from God. There is also a variety of viewpoints on who may interpret the Scriptures with authority. These range from those who insist that every Christian believer is an equally authoritative interpreter to those who argue for a collective interpretive authority by the local faith community, or by an officially appointed teaching magisterium. A conclusion of this study is that it is easier to imagine progress and enlarged consensus on the issue of *interpretive authority* among the traditions than to resolve differences over the *interpretive methods* to be employed.

D. *The Church as the Community of Faithful Worship, Witness, and Service in the World*

All of the traditions represented in our study are communal and understand the church to be the body of Christ, God's sacramental blessing in the world, and a community of prayer, preaching, healing, and teaching. The church also is a community of witness for the salvation of all who hear and respond in faith. It is a community gathered and empowered by the Spirit, one in solidarity with the poor and oppressed who struggle for justice and peace. This plurality of images is required to suggest the variety of ways Christian people understand the essence of the church. It likewise is necessary in order not to obscure its functions shared throughout history, namely, ordered worship, preaching, teaching, communal life in service to the needs of people within and outside the church, faithful administration, stewardship of resources, evangelism, and mission.

Christian communities are bearers of tradition. This tradition finds expression in liturgies, prayers, and hymns, as well as in the actions of councils, synods, bishops, and popes, and the insights of theologians, saints, martyrs, mystics, and other witnesses among the faithful. Although the older church communities affirmed the continuity of tradition, the Protestant reforming movements of the sixteenth century invoked ancient tradition in order to restore the primacy of the scriptural word. They then began building new traditions as part of their communal experience of faith. Even restorationist and primitivist Christian movements invoke and create traditions that then take on a normative quality, in spite of the fact that their beliefs do not readily accommodate such a view of tradition.

The relative importance of Scripture and tradition and the proper method for invoking the authority of tradition remain in dispute, however. Greater unity of method can be seen between Roman Catholic and Protestant churches since the Second Vatican Council. But important differences remain. Protestants sometimes fear that the Roman Catholic tradition will unduly control teaching and preaching in the church as it becomes more biblically oriented. And Roman Catholics sometimes express fear that Protestant biblical preoccupation will continue to hinder a fuller reception of tradition and the guidance of the Spirit. Many Protestants will continue to emphasize an individual or local/communal authority for interpreting tradition. Roman Catholic, Orthodox, and some Protestant Christians also will continue to emphasize a more formalized office or standing body as the authoritative interpreter. Orthodox communities understand their traditional grounding in a more richly unified manner (ancient *and* contemporary, worship *and* belief, life *and* faith) than they find in either the Roman Catholic or Protestant views of tradition.

2. Dimensions of the Apostolic Faith Shared by Some Member Traditions of the Christian Family, But Not by All

A. *Normative Creedal and Confessional Statements*

These statements comprise important substantive and procedural criteria for discerning faithfulness to the apostolic witness. Creeds summarize in highly compact and symbolic terms faith understandings arising from particular historical challenges and needs. Creeds are often employed liturgically as the communal response to the preached word, or as part of the eucharistic action. Confessions are typically longer than creeds, more discursive, and may be more clearly attuned to particular historical circumstances. They often are intended as a fuller and more precise account of the faith than may be found in creedal statements. Typically creeds are more ancient. Confessions are more representative of the emergence of the Protestant traditions.

Many churches employ ancient and modern creedal and confessional statements in worship and in catechetical formation. In some churches pastors and teachers develop their sermons and theological writings directly on the basis of confessional statements. Some churches honor and liturgically employ ancient as well as modern creedal statements while not regarding their content in a formally normative manner. Other churches, however, consider creedal or confessional statements as unwarranted intrusions between the scriptural Word (or the Holy Spirit) and the believer. "No creed but Christ" has been a byword for many such groups. But even these noncreedal churches may employ brief statements of faith in baptism or in other aspects of worship.

B. Normative Teaching Offices and Normative Polities

An authoritative person, office, or body in many churches bears responsibility for maintaining the fidelity of the church to its calling and character. For some the office of bishop bears this responsibility. Bishops together, or with a patriarch or the pope, hold final authority in determining matters of faith and morals. Other churches, however, locate this authority in different persons or standing bodies, not in an episcopal office. There is still an episcopal *function* in these churches but without that title. Among these are the following:

1. the local community of faith (churches holding a congregational polity);
2. a delegated regional and national framework of legally constituted deliberative bodies (churches holding a presbyterial polity).

These independent, congregational, and presbyterial bodies often have regional officers who fulfill quasi-episcopal pastoral functions in relation to the churches and clergy of their region. But it is clearly understood that they are *not* the teaching magisterium in these churches. The magisterial episcopacy, in its full range of symbolic, pastoral, and teaching functions seems so central to the heritage of the episcopal communions that they can scarcely imagine how others have managed without it. Surely apostolic fidelity would seem better served by such an office than in its absence. The nonepiscopal churches, however, view their own procedures as more likely to ensure faithfulness to the apostolic teaching because the gifts of the authoritative Word and Spirit are believed to be mediated through personal, pastoral, and ecclesial encounters and not through an episcopal office where undue centralized authority might be exercised. In the process of receiving the World Council of Churches' Lima Document entitled *Baptism, Eucharist and Ministry* (BEM, 1982), of working through the Consultation on Church Unity's *Consensus*, and of moving toward a common confession of the apostolic faith, these matters are of particular importance.

C. *Normative Experience of Conversion, Sanctification, Holiness, Liberation*

Many Christian bodies understand their apostolic fidelity to be grounded in acts of love and justice, in a life of peace, in missionary outreach, in service to all in need, in a personal confession of Jesus Christ as Lord and Savior, and in solidarity with the poor and the oppressed. Some groups emphasize a more personal holiness. Others are Spirit led. Still others are more mission oriented. Discipleship in Jesus Christ and following in his way are often the central expressions of fidelity. The historic peace churches would be included in this group, along with holiness, restorationist, and Spirit-led movements. Churches and base ecclesial communities among the poor, oppressed, and racial/ethnic minority groups would also find their primary apostolic rootage here. And the sanctificationist side of the Wesleyan and Calvinist/Puritan traditions belong here as well, although other dimensions of apostolic fidelity are also present in these churches. All Christian bodies, to be sure, teach and endeavor to practice works of righteousness, love, and peace as expressions of Christian faith. But in the traditions under discussion here, a holy, serving, liberating *life* is at the heart of apostolic fidelity. In addition, many other churches in North America, and indeed over the globe, are actively working on behalf of racial justice, peace, and nuclear disarmament, the alleviation of poverty and hunger, justice for women, and other social issues. All these churches, whatever their diverse ecclesial traditions, would identify their work for justice as part of their apostolic fidelity and would resist any definition of apostolicity that did not take full account of such life and work.

RECOMMENDATIONS

The following dimensions of apostolic fidelity, it seems, hold promise for greater unity of understanding and practice in the ecumenical family:
• the confession of Jesus Christ as God and Savior;
• the authoritative witness of the Scriptures;
• the guidance and inspiration of the Holy Spirit;
• the church as the community of faithful worship, witness, and service in the world.
There surely is sufficient common ground here to hope that all members of the Christian family can share enough life together that they will come to a better understanding of their diversity and be more open to enrichment from other patterns. Serious and divisive issues will remain, but they can be addressed within the community of Christian tradition that acknowledges the shared essentials of Christian faith, if not the fullness of the church, in all members of the family.

The dimensions of apostolic fidelity shared by some but not all traditions—
• normative creedal and confessional statements;
• normative teaching and episcopal offices;
• normative polities;
• normative experiences of conversion, sanctification, holiness, liberation—
seem more difficult to resolve. The fact that some churches are noncreedal or vigorously anticreedal while others regard creedal and confessional statements as normative expressions of the gospel poses a serious challenge. It is the same with authority for belief—individual conscience, local congregation, assembly, col-

lege of bishops, pope—the differences are not readily resolvable. While no tradition denies the importance of a holy life or working for the increase of justice and liberation, some traditions would locate the foundation of apostolicity there. In light of these observations, we suggest that the Commission on Faith and Order of the National Council of Churches, as it continues its work toward a common confession of the apostolic faith, in concert with the Faith and Order Commission of the World Council of Churches, consider the following recommendations:

A. Recommendations Regarding the Nicene-Constantinopolitan Creed

1. Churches that already employ the Nicene Creed in worship and faith reflection should be urged to recognize officially or adopt the Nicene Creed as the ancient and still regulative summary of the apostolic witness.
2. Churches that are noncreedal or anticreedal should be encouraged to engage in a period of sustained study of the Nicene Creed. They might also be asked to reflect on how their understanding of apostolic fidelity can find expression in the Nicene Creed, and how they might summarize their contemporary understanding of the apostolic faith.

B. Recommendations for a Contemporary Commentary on the Nicene Creed

A commentary should be prepared and recommended to the churches that discusses the meaning of the ancient formula in contemporary language, and should emphasize the following:

1. interpreting the soteriology of the creed so that the radically free and justifying grace of God in Jesus Christ would represent the foundational insights of the sixteenth-century Protestant Reformation and the twentieth-century Roman Catholic Renewal;
2. interpreting the creedal references to the church and Chris-

tian life in ways that clarify and sustain the apostolic character of a holy and sanctified life, working for justice and liberation.

C. Recommendation for Further Analysis and Study

While the classification scheme employed in this discussion emerged in the work of this apostolic faith subgroup, other categories should be explored further. One such scheme proposed is the distinction between traditions where *formal* expressions of the apostolic faith seemed foundational and traditions where *functional* expressions are at the center. Other conceptual frameworks may cast fresh light on the effort to describe the diverse expression of apostolicity in the North American scene.

We believe that implementing such recommendations would strengthen our unity and take us nearer to that time when all Christians might confess their apostolic unity in ancient and contemporary expressions.